Contents

Money and Measurements

Nineteenth-century wages and prices have been left in pounds, shillings and pence. There were 20 shillings, and 240 (old) pence, to the pound. The shilling has become our 5p piece.

Metric measurements have been used throughout the book.

Approximate equivalents

1 metre   = 3.28 feet (39.4″)
1 kilometre = 0.62 miles
1 hectare   = 2.47 acres
1 kilogram = 2.24 pounds
1 tonne   = 0.98 tons

1 The Years of Unrest

In June 1815 an army under the command of the Duke of Wellington defeated the French Emperor Napoleon at Waterloo. It was the last battle in a war which had been going on for twenty-two years. These years had been very difficult for Britain. The country's leaders had been forced to work hard to deal with the problems of fighting a long war on land and at sea. Huge sums had been spent on equipping and paying the army and navy, and thousands of men had joined the armed forces to fight against the French. Now it was over. But, if the British people expected to be able to relax and enjoy life, they were to be disappointed. They soon found that peacetime had problems too.

The monarchy

In the first place, the system of government needed to be reformed. The trouble started right at the top. The king, George III, was old, blind, deaf and mad. Since 1811 his eldest son, George the Prince Regent, had been acting as king. When he was in a good mood the prince was generous and charming, but he was selfish and hated having to follow the advice of his ministers. If he could not get his own way he would lose control of himself completely, weeping, shouting and stamping so that many of those around him feared that he might have inherited his father's madness. His private life was scandalous. He had been forced to marry a German princess, his cousin Caroline of Brunswick, whom he hated. They had a daughter, Charlotte, and as soon as she was born, they separated. George spent his time in the company of various middle-aged ladies, while Caroline travelled round Europe and became famous for her love affairs, some of them, it was said, with her own servants.

The splendour of the Royal Pavilion at Brighton, built for the Prince Regent, was a great contrast to the squalid homes of many of his subjects

The prince was very unpopular. Fortunately young Princess Charlotte was well liked. In 1816 she married and soon she became pregnant. Then disaster struck. In 1817 she died giving birth to a still-born child. This meant that once the old king and the Prince Regent were dead, the throne would go to one of the prince's brothers, all of whom were odd in one way or another. Thus, so far as the royal family was concerned, prospects were bad. It was impossible to feel any respect for them and most people probably agreed with Wellington, who described the family as 'the damnedest millstone about the necks of any government that can be imagined'.

The political system

The government itself was not particularly popular. The country was run by landowners. The king's ministers were selected from among the members of the House of Lords and the House of Commons. All the lords were land-owners, while the Commons were elected according to an out of date and corrupt system. Only property owners could sit in Parliament,

Some working people distrusted Orator Hunt because he was rich. He was also vain and arrogant. But he had great courage and was the best public speaker in Britain

and in most places the poor had no vote. (For details see Chapter 5.)

There were two political parties — the Whigs and the Tories. Many Whigs were in favour of reforming the system, but it was more than thirty years since there had been a majority of Whig members in the House of Commons. In 1815 the Tories were firmly in power. Most of them were opposed to reform. The Prime Minister, Lord Liverpool, had few ideas. He spent most of his time making sure that his ministers worked smoothly together. The strongest members of the government were Lord Eldon and Lord Castlereagh. Eldon was Lord Chancellor, and was in charge of the judges and magistrates. Castlereagh was Foreign Secretary. Both were against reform, and were very unpopular. So was the Home Secretary, Lord Sidmouth, because it was his job to keep order in the country and to see that government decisions were carried out.

The radicals

The majority of the population had no say in the way in which their country was governed. Many people thought this unfair, and a few politicians believed that all men ought to have the right to vote. People who wanted to make such important changes in the system were called radicals. There was only a handful of them in Parliament, but others spent their time touring the country addressing meetings to try to persuade those present to sign petitions and join in demonstrations in favour of reform. The most famous agitator was Henry Hunt, the son of a prosperous Wiltshire farmer. 'Orator' Hunt was tall and handsome. He was easy to pick out in a crowd because he always wore a white top hat. As a rule his manner was quiet and gentlemanly, but when he began to speak he changed. There were no microphones or loudspeakers, and in the effort to make his voice heard and understood by a large crowd he bellowed as loud as he could, his eyes bulged, his face swelled and his fists clenched with a kind of 'painful energy'. His message was always the same: that all the country's evils were due to the unfair and corrupt system of government.

The same message was put across by a famous writer, William Cobbett. The son of a Surrey farm labourer, he had served in the army and had lived for a time in France and America, both of which were republics. He had spent little time at school, and had learned to rely on his own common sense and judgement, even when most people disagreed with him. He had no time for politicians and scholars, but he respected practical down-to-earth farmers, and had great sympathy for ordinary working countrymen. He ran a magazine called the *Political Register*, written in plain English which everybody could understand. In 1810 he had been imprisoned for two years for writing an article attacking the army for bringing in German troops to flog some English soldiers. This made him very popular, and working men clubbed together to buy and read the *Political Register*.

Such men as Cobbett, Hunt and their supporters alarmed the government, most of whom had never got over the shock of the French Revolution, in which the French king and many of the nobility had been executed. They feared that any reform of the system in Britain might also lead to a violent revolution resulting in chaos and bloodshed. If there was disorder, they could do very little. There was no regular police force. To restore order the authorities therefore had to call in the army. This had two disadvantages. First, if there were no troops anywhere near, it might take several days to move in enough soldiers to control the riot. Next, the troops usually treated rioters as if they were an enemy army and charged them down with swords and bayonets, causing many casualties. This made the government more unpopular than ever.

COBBETT's WEEKLY POLITICAL REGISTER.

Vol. 32, N° 9.]--LONDON, SATURDAY, MARCH 1, 1817.-[Price 1s.½d.

257]   [258

A LETTER
TO ALL
TRUE-HEARTED ENGLISHMEN.
The Suspension of the Habeas Corpus Act.—The Sedition Bills.—The Petition of Mr. Cleary—The Petition of Mr. Hunt.—The Defence of Annual Parliaments and Universal Suffrage by the Duke of Richmond.

London, 25th February, 1817.

Countrymen and Friends,

Before this Letter will reach your hands, acts of Parliament of the most tremendous importance to us all will probably be passed, such acts being at this moment before the House of Commons in the shape of *Bills*; from which shape they are changed into laws in a few days, and which laws most deeply affect our liberties and lives.

I will first explain clearly what the *Habeas Corpus Act* is. You all know

man could be seized and sent to prison without these precautions, who would be safe? And, in order that this most necessary law may be duly attended to, there is another law for preventing any neglect of the observance of all these matters; and this law is usually called the *Habeas Corpus Act*. It is so called because the *writ*, which I shall speak of presently, begins with these two Latin words, *Habeas Corpus*. This act enables any man who may be put into any prison, or confined in any manner, to apply to a Judge for what is called a *writ*, or command, to bring such man before the Judge, that the Judge may hear his complaint; and then the Judge, if he finds that the man has been sent to prison, or confined, *without all the necessary evidence and forms before mentioned*, is obliged to order the prisoner to be discharged; and the prisoner may then prosecute

Papers and magazines like the Political Register *had no pictures and used only small type. This makes them look very unattractive today*

3

To add to their difficulties, the government had very little idea of what ordinary working men were thinking. To get information the Home Office employed spies who attended political meetings and sent in reports. These spies were expected to warn government of any plots. Some, known as *agents provocateurs*, went further. They encouraged discontent and offered to help those who were plotting against the government. Then, when they had enough evidence, they informed the authorities and the plotters were arrested and punished. Spies always exaggerated the number and importance of the plots which they discovered. As a result, the government usually believed the situation to be more dangerous than it really was.

Causes of distress

Changes in the countryside

There was a good deal of distress and discontent in Britain between 1815 and 1820. Some of this was due to a new system of farming (see Chapter 4) which meant that labourers were worse off. In the old days they had been given food and lodging as well as a money wage. Under the new system they were paid entirely in cash. Their wages were often so low that they had difficulty in making a living, especially when food prices were high. To make matters worse, the population in the countryside was rising. This meant that there were not enough jobs to go round and labourers had to leave their villages and tramp to the towns to look for work.

The growth of factories

From 1780 onwards the number of factories in Britain increased enormously (see Chapter 3). These factories produced goods, especially cloth, much more cheaply than a man working at home. This meant that many craftsmen, like hand-loom weavers, were either thrown out of work or had to reduce their prices so much that they could no longer make a decent living. Such men were bitter and angry and were easily persuaded to join in plots against the govern-

ment. Some farmworkers were also worse off because of the growth of factories. In the past they had been able to earn extra money by making cloth in their spare time. But now the factories could do it cheaper, and they could no longer sell what they produced. Even those who were working in the factories had some cause to grumble. When trade was good they were well paid, but in bad times their pay was reduced or else they were dismissed. If the factory did not want their work, they faced complete ruin. They had no land to grow their own food and no hope of getting a job anywhere else. Thus, when trade was bad, factory workers suffered great hardships.

The end of the war

Once the war was over, hard times were not long in coming. For many years factories in Britain had been busy producing supplies for the army and navy. With the coming of peace, these supplies were no longer needed and many men and women lost their jobs. They were joined in their search for work by thousands of men discharged from the forces. The government made matters worse. To help to pay for the war they had introduced income tax, which they had promised to abolish as soon as the war ended. They had also borrowed huge sums of money. At the end of the war they kept their promise to abolish income tax and found that there was not enough money coming in to run the country and pay interest on what they had borrowed. To make up the amount they needed, they put more and more taxes on the things people bought until, in 1820, Sydney Smith complained that there were 'taxes upon every article which enters into the mouth, or covers the back, or is placed under the foot'. He went on to paint a vivid picture of a sick Englishman lying on his bed 'which has paid 22 per cent, pouring his medicine which has paid 7 per cent into a spoon which has paid 15 per cent'. It was comparatively easy for the rich to pay taxes on everyday items. For the poor it was a different matter and many of them were paying half their wages in taxes of one sort or another. Yet, they had no vote and thus no say in how all this money was spent.

The hard work of the poor keeps the rich in comfort and plenty

The Corn Law

In 1815 there were various laws in force which were deeply resented by many ordinary people. The Game Laws made it illegal for hungry labourers to catch and eat rabbits, hares and other game, while the criminal law laid down very severe penalties for minor crimes like thefts of small sums of money. But the most unpopular Act of all was the Corn Law.

In 1815 most British farmers were very prosperous because they had been able to sell their crops for high prices for many years past. They now feared that the good times might be coming to an end. In 1813 there had been an enormous harvest and the price of wheat had fallen to about seventy shillings a quarter. In

1814 the crop was poor but, with the war at an end, wheat was imported from abroad and the price stayed down. This worried many farmers, because during the years when prices had been high, some of them had paid huge sums of money for land and had spent a lot improving poor soil to make it fit for cultivation. They argued that they could not make money growing wheat unless its price was eighty shillings a quarter or more, and appealed to Parliament for help. Such a price would mean dear bread for the rest of the country but in 1815 most Members of Parliament were either landowners themselves or else were elected by landowners. As a result, they listened to the farmers and passed a law which made it illegal to import foreign wheat until the price of English

The unfortunate Englishman is crushed under the weight of his taxes, while the high price of bread puts it out of his reach

wheat reached eighty shillings a quarter. They hoped that this law, known as the Corn Law of 1815, would keep wheat prices high, so that farmers would remain prosperous. But high wheat prices also meant that bread would be expensive and working men hated the thought that they were having to buy dear bread in order to put money in the pockets of the farmers.

So there were good reasons for people to feel discontented. But as long as they had work and could afford enough to eat, most of them did not bother to go to meetings, sign petitions and attend demonstrations to try to bring about reforms. When trade was slack and prices rose, on the other hand, they would meet, march and demonstrate. Sometimes, when times were really hard, a few were even prepared to use force. When bread was dear, blood was cheap.

Meetings and riots

Spa Fields

The first real trouble came in 1816. All over northern Europe the harvest was poor and food prices high. There was little money to spare for buying manufactured goods, so trade was slack and many factories laid off workers. Whole families found themselves faced with poverty and hunger. In the north there were strikes and some riots when firms tried to reduce wages. In a pamphlet published in November, Cobbett claimed that the cause of their 'present miseries' was 'the enormous amount of the taxes which the government compelled them to pay'. Major Cartwright, a radical leader who had been active since 1776, set up a chain of Hampden Clubs, named after a seventeenth-century gentleman who had refused to pay a tax which

6

he believed to be illegal. These clubs, open to anyone willing to pay a penny a week, organised local and national events. The most important of these took place on 15 November, when a huge meeting was held at Spa Fields in London. Silk weavers who had lost their jobs because trade was slack went to the meeting. So did sailors who had been discharged from the navy and could not find work.

A very big crowd gathered to hear an address by Orator Hunt. In a rousing speech he claimed that unemployment was caused by high taxes, and that high taxes were caused by corruption. The meeting was a great success, and another was summoned for 2 December at the same place. Hunt wanted to draw up a petition to the Prince Regent, but some of his supporters, including James Watson and Arthur Thistlewood, decided to try to start an armed rebellion. They were encouraged by a government spy named Castle. On 2 December they went to Spa Fields before Hunt and led some of the crowd away to rampage through London. They broke into gunsmiths' shops, stole weapons, and marched on the Tower of London where they tried in vain to persuade the soldiers on guard to join them. In the end the authorities, who had been warned by Castle to expect trouble, easily restored order.

The Spa Fields riot had important results. The sight of a 'reforming' mob marching through the streets of London frightened many respectable middle-class people and made them determined to oppose reform. The violence also gave the government a good excuse to clamp down on the radicals. To make matters worse, in January 1817 the Prince Regent's coach was mobbed at the state opening of Parliament, and one of its windows was broken. When the Commons debated the situation, they were told of plots to seize the Bank of England and the Tower of London. They decided that something must be done. Accordingly, they passed an Act forbidding meetings which might encourage people to revolt against the government. They also suspended the Habeas Corpus Act. This was a seventeenth-century law which gave everybody held in prison the right to be brought to trial. Once the Act was suspended, the authorities could keep people in prison for as long as they liked without trying them, and in fact about fifty men were imprisoned without trial in 1817. Cobbett was convinced that he would be arrested and fled to America. In 1818 the suspension of Habeas Corpus ended, and in 1819 Cobbett returned to Britain.

The Blanketeers

In spite of these measures, there was more trouble in 1817, most of it in the Midlands and north of England. In March a number of working men, most of them weavers, set out from Manchester to march to London and petition the government. Since the march would take several days each man carried his own blanket to wrap up in at night. The leaders expected men from Yorkshire and the Midlands to join them. One told his followers that if they could reach Birmingham they would be 100,000 strong. In fact the 'Blanketeers', as they were called, only got as far as north Staffordshire. They were dispersed by troops and more than 200 were arrested.

The Pentrich rising

In the summer, there was another, much more violent outbreak. During the spring there had been a good deal of plotting. Much of it was in the north and Midlands, where many craftsmen had been thrown out of work by the new factories. There had already been a good deal of violence in the area, with gangs of men attacking factories and smashing machines. These gangs were called Luddites because their leaders signed all their orders and letters 'General Ludd', so that nobody would know their real names. The worst Luddite riots were in 1811 and 1812, but in 1817 there were still plenty of men who felt that the whole system of government was so rotten and corrupt that it ought to be destroyed by force. They soon drew up plans for a huge armed rebellion, timed to take place at the beginning of June. But one of the plotters was a government spy named Oliver who sent back detailed reports to the Home Secretary in London. Most of the leaders

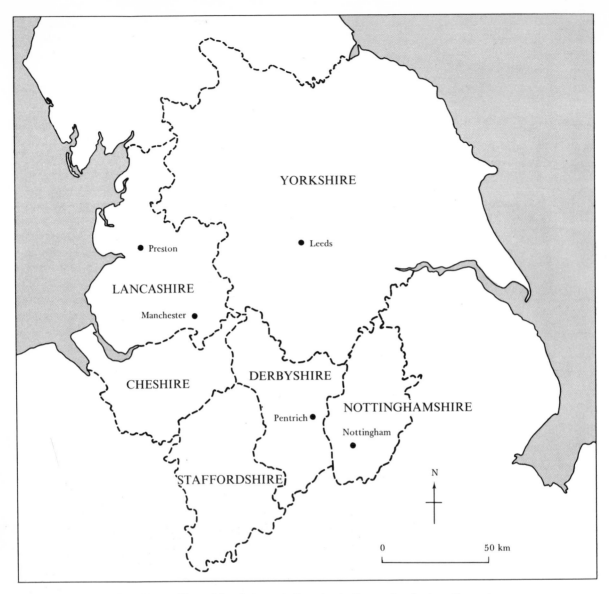

This map shows the places affected by riots and disorder in the early nineteenth century

discovered just in time what Oliver was doing and abandoned their plans. Unfortunately the Derbyshire leader, Jeremy Brandreth, an unemployed stocking weaver from Pentrich, could not be told in time. On 9 June he collected together two or three hundred men and prepared to march south. He told his followers that they would easily capture Nottingham and then march with thousands of others to London, set up a provisional government and wipe off the National Debt. He and his men set off in the rain to round up more support from nearby farms. At one of them Brandreth fired a shot through a window and killed a servant. Few men joined them. As they approached Nottingham the small band met a troop of Hussars. At once the rioters dropped their weapons and fled. Many of them were captured: thirty-five were tried. Four, including Brandreth, were hanged.

Troubles in Scotland

Scotland, too, had its problems in 1816. One of Cartwright's Hampden Clubs was founded in Glasgow and a government spy named Richmond told Kirkman Finlay, the city's MP, that the members of the club had sworn illegal oaths and were about to launch a rebellion. Finlay told the Lord Advocate, and several Glasgow radicals were arrested. In 1817 they were tried. The result embarrassed the government. It turned out that the club members were solid, respectable men who had no intention of rebelling against the government. Only two of them were convicted, and they were sentenced to six months in prison. To make matters worse, a paper called *The Leeds Mercury* published a number of articles which for the first time told the public how the Home Office spy system worked. These articles made many people very

uneasy, and it became difficult to get juries to convict if they thought that the evidence against a prisoner came from a government spy.

Peterloo

Fortunately, the harvest of 1817 was good, trade improved, and the number of those out of work fell. This meant that in 1818 there was much less discontent and no disorder, apart from some strikes in the north. The men who had been imprisoned after the suspension of the Habeas Corpus Act were released, and the government relaxed. But it was not to last. In 1819 trade slumped once again and demands for some kind of demonstration increased. The radical leaders had learned from what had happened in 1816 and 1817. They were determined that this time there was to be no violence. Peace, cleanliness, sobriety and order

An officer encourages his well-fed troops to attack the poor at Peterloo: 'Down with 'em! Chop 'em down, my brave boys'

were to be their watchwords. The most important meeting of the year was to take place on Monday 16 August at St Peter's Fields in Manchester. Fifty thousand people were expected to attend, and to make sure that they would be able to enter and leave the meeting place in a quick and orderly way, the various contingents were drilled by men who had served in the army during the war. In glorious weather the local groups set off for Manchester, each led by its commander wearing a sprig of laurel in his hat. Some of the men carried staves over their shoulders. Many of them took their wives and children with them. All were dressed in their Sunday best, and looked forward to hearing a speech from Orator Hunt himself.

The authorities knew that the meeting was to take place. They were very alarmed indeed by all the marching and drilling. They feared that this might mean an armed revolt was planned. The local magistrates wanted to take no chances, and decided to arrest Hunt before he could make his speech. To do this they had a number of regular mounted troops standing by. They also had a detachment of local yeomanry. These were volunteer, part-time cavalrymen. They were all wealthy, and most of them hated and feared the radicals.

As Hunt was escorted by his friends to the platform to address the meeting, the magistrates told some of the troops to go in and arrest him. The soldiers were pushed and jostled by the crowd, and the magistrates ordered the rest of the troops to go in and disperse the crowd. The soldiers drew their swords and charged. The people tried to run out of their way, but they were so tightly packed that they could not move. So the troops rode over them, hacking at heads and limbs with their swords. The air was filled with shouts, screams, curses and prayers as the huge crowd struggled to get clear from the charging troops. The yeomanry were worse than the soldiers, attacking sections of the crowd who were hemmed into a corner and unable to get away.

Eventually the field was cleared. Eleven people had been killed and about four hundred injured. The platform remained 'with a few broken flag-staves and a torn and gashed ban-

ner or two dropping, while over the whole field were strewed caps, bonnets, hats, shawls and shoes, trampled, torn and bloody'. The last blow was struck by General Clay. He saw Orator Hunt, under arrest, being escorted up the steps of a magistrate's house and hit him so hard on the head that he flattened the famous white hat over Hunt's face.

The massacre of St Peter's Fields roused strong feelings. The Prince Regent sent a message to the magistrates congratulating them on their action, but many people were shocked by what had happened. The radicals felt that the British army, which won glory at Waterloo, was disgraced by the action at St Peter's Fields, and nicknamed the incident 'Peterloo'. They discussed what they ought to do next. Some were in favour of an armed revolt, and began to manufacture pikes out of wooden staves and knive blades. Others organised meetings to protest at what had happened, and when Orator Hunt was released on bail and travelled to London, he was greeted by huge cheering crowds.

The Six Acts

All this activity alarmed the government. They feared that the authorities had not got enough power to keep the radicals under control. Parliament therefore passed the Six Acts. The first made it illegal for bands of civilians to march and drill like soldiers. The second prohibited all public meetings larger than fifty people, unless they all came from the parish in which the meeting was held. The third enabled magistrates to search for arms without a warrant, and the fourth made it easier for them to seize seditious literature. The fifth allowed more cases to be tried by a magistrate without a jury, and the sixth increased the stamp duty on newspapers, so that they now cost about sixpence each. After the Six Acts it was impossible for the radicals to hold any more of their huge meetings, and it was much easier for magistrates to search their premises and to put them on trial. A large number of radical leaders were arrested and imprisoned and the danger of revolt seemed to pass.

As police burst in to arrest the Cato Street Conspirators, one tries to escape through the roof, another douses a candle with his hat, while a third stabs and kills one of the officers

The Cato Street Conspiracy

There were still two shocks for the government, however. In London Arthur Thistlewood, who had played a leading part in the Spa Fields riot, planned to murder the whole Cabinet as they sat at dinner. Thistlewood, who was encouraged by a government spy named Edwards, hoped that this would serve as a signal for a country-wide rebellion. He and his fellow-conspirators had a good stock of weapons at their London headquarters, a stable loft in Cato Street, but on 23 February 1820 the house was raided by a number of police and soldiers. In the struggle most of the gang were captured and a policeman was killed. In due course eleven of the gang were put on trial for treason. Six were transported. Five, including Thistlewood, were sentenced to be hanged and then beheaded. Before he was sentenced one of them, John Brunt, a shoemaker, told the court how he had become involved in the plot. He

said that at one time he had been able to earn about £3 or £4 a week, and 'while this was the case, he never meddled with politics, but when he found his income reduced to ten shillings a week, he began to look about him. And what did he find? Why, men in power who met to starve and plunder the country.' He was not sorry for what he had planned to do. 'He would have gone through with it to the very bottom. He would die as the descendant of an ancient Briton.' On 28 April the five were hanged in front of an enormous crowd which booed the executioner and bellowed, 'Bring out Edwards.'

The Radical War

While the Cato Street Conspirators were in prison waiting to be tried, there was trouble in Scotland and in parts of the north of England. There were rumours that a great rising was to take place all over Britian at the beginning of

April, and in the north of England a few bands of men gathered together, only to go home again when they realised how small their numbers were. In Scotland bills were posted in Glasgow calling on people to revolt. Many weavers, whose pay had been falling over the years, went on strike, and a small armed band marched from Strathaven in Lanarkshire to the outskirts of Glasgow, where they expected to find a huge army of supporters. They found nobody, and went home. A few Calton weavers set out to seize the Carron ironworks but at Bonnymuir, near Falkirk, they were attacked and scattered by mounted troops. Forty-seven men were arrested and tried. Three of these, James Wilson, John Baird and Andrew Hardie, were executed.

The queen's affair

By the early summer all this excitement was over. This was just as well, because the government had to deal with a crisis in the royal family. At the beginning of 1820 the old king died, and the Prince Regent succeeded to the throne as King George IV. He was determined that Caroline should not become queen, and asked his ministers to get him a divorce. Caroline decided to fight the divorce, and the case was tried by the House of Lords. The trial dragged on for several months, but in the end the government decided that the evidence was not clear enough and dropped the case. At George's coronation Caroline tried to enter the Abbey to be crowned with him, but was turned away at the door. A month later she died. George was delighted.

From time to time between 1815 and 1820 Britain had seemed to be quite close to a violent revolution. The next few years were to be different, with little or no unrest or disorder. There were two reasons for this. First, trade was good, work was plentiful and wages were high. Second, the Tory government introduced a number of reforms which made life better for at least some ordinary people.

2 The Dawn of Reform

Changes in the government

After 1821 there were several important changes in the government. In January 1822, the Home Secretary, Lord Sidmouth, resigned, and was replaced by Robert Peel, a brilliantly clever man who was determined to improve the way in which the criminal law worked. In August the Foreign Secretary, Lord Castlereagh, a convinced opponent of all reform, committed suicide, and was replaced by George Canning, who was in favour of making limited changes where they were really needed. Finally, in January 1823, F. J. Robinson became Chancellor of the Exchequer, and William Huskisson came into the government as President of the Board of Trade. Both these men had a good understanding of finance, and were able to persuade the rest of the Cabinet to allow them to bring in various reforms to improve trade and to make the system of taxation a little less unfair.

Peel at the Home Office

Robert Peel, the new Home Secretary, had a difficult job. The police force was badly organised and untrained. This meant that most crimes were never solved. Criminals therefore ran little risk of being caught and put on trial.

The convicts kept in these hulks at Woolwich worked in the nearby arsenal making munitions

To try to dicourage them, the law laid down very severe penalties for those who were caught. In 1815 more than two hundred offences were punishable by hanging. These included stealing five shillings or more from a shop, impersonating Chelsea pensioners and damaging Westminster Bridge, as well as a host of more serious crimes.

This approach did not work. Clever and experienced criminals escaped. Only the young and stupid were caught and tried. Many were hanged but often the sentence was commuted to transportation or imprisonment. Indeed, it was reckoned that only about 10 per cent of those sentenced to death were executed. Peel could see that there was no point in laying down the death penalty for offences when offenders knew that it was unlikely that they would be hanged. He believed that quite mild punishments would prevent people from committing crimes as long as they were fairly sure that they would be caught. He wanted on the one hand to make the law less severe and on the other to make the police more efficient.

Criminal law reform

Peel first set to work to reform the law. Some progress had already been made. In 1808 Sir Samuel Romilly persuaded Parliament to alter the penalty for picking pockets from death to transportation for life. Between 1813 and 1818 Romilly had also tried several times to reduce the punishment for stealing five shillings from a shop. The Commons had agreed but the Lords had refused to alter the law. Finally in 1818 the Commons had appointed a committee to investigate all offences which carried the death penalty. This committee recommended that about a hundred of these should be abolished, but nothing was done until Peel took over as Home Secretary. In 1823 he persuaded Parliament to do as the committee had advised and abolish a hundred capital offences. The number of people committing these crimes did not greatly increase. In 1832, therefore, after Peel had left the Home Office, hanging was abolished for a further hundred offences. The process continued. After 1838 no one was hanged except for treason, murder or attempted murder.

Transportation

The fact that fewer criminals were hanged meant that more than before had to be punished in other ways. Many were transported to the colonies, especially Australia. Transportation was for seven years, fourteen years or for life. Once they reached Australia, the convicts were either kept in a government gang to work on jobs like roadmaking, or 'assigned' to a farmer to work for him as labourers. Once his sentence was over a convict was free to return to Britain but only a small number did so. The rest preferred to remain in Australia, where some of them became very rich.

Peel doubted if criminals really feared transportation as a punishment. It is true that the government labour gangs were very strictly controlled, while convicts found guilty of further offences in Australia were sent to penal settlements where they had to work chained together in gangs. The work was very heavy and they were not allowed to speak. If they did anything wrong they were mercilessly flogged. At the other end of the scale, however, a convict lucky enough to be assigned to a good master was very well off. One of them wrote home in 1845 describing himself as 'very comfortable indeed' and 'doing a great deal better than ever I was at home'. These differences worried Peel, and he tried to make transportation a more effective punishment by increasing the number of convicts working in government gangs and by supervising those who were working for farmers. This did not suit the colonists who wanted to be able to use the convict labour as they thought best. There were also arguments over who should pay the cost of convict settlements. The two sides were unable to agree and the system of transportation was slowly run down. The last convict ship sailed from Britain in 1867. In all about 162,000 prisoners had been transported.

Prison conditions

The fact that fewer criminals were executed or transported meant that more people were imprisoned for long periods in Britain. In the

The convict in this cell at Pentonville prison slept on a hammock bed. During the day the hammock was taken down and the prisoner worked at his loom

eighteenth and early nineteenth centuries every county ran its own prisons and they were often disgracefully neglected. During the day prisoners of all kinds mingled together in common rooms or open courts. Young people awaiting trial and debtors were thrown in with hardened criminals and prostitutes. The cells were filthy, damp and over-run with vermin. Poor prisoners rarely had enough to eat. Those with money could hire better accommodation and buy plenty to eat and drink. Their money went straight into the pocket of the jailer, who made a good living from the fees he got from the prisoners.

John Howard, who visited many British jails, described Coventry prison in 1782 as having

four dungeons about 9 feet by 6; at the upper corner of each, a little window, 11 inches by 7. All are very damp, dirty and offensive. Only one court for all prisoners. No straw, no infirmary, no bath.

15

Holloway prison. On the right prisoners are at work on the treadmill. Those sitting in the stalls are unpicking rope

He found one man there who had been pardoned nine months previously, but was still imprisoned because he had no money to pay fees demanded by the jailer and by the lawyers who had drawn up his pardon.

In 1777 Howard published his findings in a book called *The State of English Prisons*, which so shocked Parliament that Acts were passed ordering that different classes of prisoners should be kept apart, and instructing magistrates to inspect prisons regularly. Unfortunately many counties ignored these Acts, and when Elizabeth Fry began visiting prisons in 1812, conditions were still almost as bad as ever. At Newgate prison in London she found 300 women prisoners of all sorts crowded together in two wards and two cells. There was no bedding, so they all had to sleep on the floor. Everything was filthy and the whole place stank. The women could buy drink, and some of them were drunk for much of the time, shout-

ing and swearing at one another and begging for money from visitors.

Elizabeth decided that something must be done. She therefore organised a committee with twelve members who volunteered to work with the Newgate prisoners. They set up a school and provided work for the women to do. Within a short time the place was clean, quiet and orderly.

Elizabeth Fry's work became very well known, and politicians and philosophers began to demand fundamental changes in the whole prison system. Three things particularly worried them. Prisons were not properly supervised, and all sorts of prisoners mixed together, which meant that old and experienced criminals had a very bad influence on younger and less experienced convicts. Finally, in most prisons no attempt was made to give prisoners any work. Many people argued that if only convicts were made to work hard, they would get into

16

the habit of regular work and would then be more likely to take a steady job when they left prison. At the same time, the knowledge that a prison sentence involved hard work might act as a deterrent to others.

Prison reform

Peel agreed with all these criticisms, and in 1823 he began to reform the system. He ordered magistrates to see that prisoners were divided up so that hardened criminals would not be able to corrupt the others. He made sure that magistrates inspected their prisons regularly, and sent their reports to him. He ordered regular salaries to be paid to jailers, so that they no longer had to rely on fees for a living. Peel was only partly successful in his work. He still had to work through the local magistrates, and if they chose to ignore his instructions, there was little he could do. In 1835 the Home Office appointed its own prison inspectors to go round the country, but it was not until 1878 that all prisons were brought under direct government control.

Meanwhile, great changes were taking place in the treatment of convicts. In some prisons the authorities went to a great deal of trouble to make sure that convicts would never meet face to face. They were kept alone in their cells for most of the time, and when they met other convicts they had their faces covered by a kind of mask. Even their chapels were built so that once a prisoner was in his place he could see nobody but the clergyman. This treatment was known as the separate system, and was designed to prevent convicts having a bad influence on one another. For the same reason, some prisons organised a 'silent' system, under which inmates were allowed to mix together, but were not allowed to speak. This was very difficult to enforce—some prisoners quickly learned to speak without moving their lips, while others devised various forms of sign language.

By the middle of the nineteenth century most prisoners had to work during their sentence. Some unpicked old ropes. Others made mats or wove cloth. Those sentenced to hard labour often had to work a treadmill. In some prisons

the mill pumped water into storage tanks. In others it worked huge fans. Prisoners called this 'grinding the air'. In prisons operating the separate system there were often hand cranks in the cells which rotated a number of blades on a shaft in a box of sand. Each prisoner was expected to turn the handle 10,000 times a day, which took about eight hours. Young prisoners were sometimes given shot drill, which meant constantly lifting and setting down heavy iron cannon balls.

Convicts who made trouble while in prison were punished. For minor faults they lost part or all of their meals for a day or two. More serious offences were punished by a few days in a dark cell, a room in which there was not a single chink of light. Most prisoners feared these punishments and behaved, but if they continued to break the rules, they could be taken before magistrates who might order them to be flogged.

Most of the old prison buildings were quite unsuitable for the new systems of treatment. Many new prisons therefore had to be built, some of which are still in use, often containing far more prisoners than their designers intended over a hundred years ago. This fact alone shows that the changes which Peel and his supporters brought about in the prison system were not the answer to crime. In spite of all that was done to make prisons tough and disagreeable, many released convicts went back to a life of crime and in due course found themselves back inside.

Peel and the police

Peel also tackled the difficult job of trying to improve the police force. The position was particularly bad in London where there were at least three different kinds of police. The City of London had its own force which patrolled only within the boundaries of the old city. Some magistrates' courts employed police. In 1822 the most famous court, Bow Street, had eight policemen, known as 'runners'. Two spent their time protecting the king, while the remainder could at any time be sent out of London on cases. In addition, each parish had its own constable—an elected, unpaid official whose

Watchmen with their lanterns, staffs and rattles were often figures of fun. This print of a fashionable man tipping over a watchman in his hut was enormously popular when it first appeared in 1821

main job was to organise watchmen to patrol the streets during the hours of darkness. These watchmen were poorly paid and badly trained. Some added to their pay by taking bribes from criminals. Even those who were keen and active would not usually chase a suspect once he had crossed the boundary into the next parish. Thus any criminal who was quick on his feet and knew his way about could easily avoid capture.

Several committees had investigated the police system. They had all agreed that it did not work, but they feared that if a really efficient force was established, it might be used by the government to control ordinary people in their everyday life. But eventually they realised that something had to be done, and in 1829 Peel set up a new police force for London. He called this the Metropolitan Police. Peel recruited men of good character, trained them properly, and paid them well. They were to wear uniform

and to be armed only with staves. To begin with the peelers or bobbies, as they were called, were very unpopular. They were only accepted when Londoners realised that the criminals had moved out to other towns where there were fewer police and a life of crime was easier. In 1839 the government passed an Act allowing other areas to set up the same kind of force. Gradually the London system was copied all over the country. Life was more difficult for criminals, and once a proper police force was established it was no longer necessary to bring in troops to control riots and disorder.

Trade union reform

The Combination Laws

In 1824 and 1825 important changes were made in the laws controlling trade unions. In 1799 and 1800 the government had feared that

One of Sir Robert Peel's new uniformed police force salutes him as he enters the House of Commons

it might be dangerous to allow workmen to 'combine' together to press for shorter hours and better pay. In the first place, they might organise disorderly demonstrations. More important, they might use their growing strength to demand changes in the system of government which might, in turn, lead to confusion and bloodshed. The government had therefore passed two Acts, known as the Combination Acts, which made all those who combined together to alter hours of work and rates of pay liable to three months' imprisonment.

These laws were never very effective. For instance, many workers joined Friendly Societies, whose members paid a few pence every week into a fund on which they could draw if they were ill or unemployed. These Friendly Societies were quite legal, but their meetings were often used to discuss how to improve wages and conditions of work. By 1824 many people were convinced that the Combi-

nation Acts were of no use. They irritated the workers without preventing them from 'combining' if they wished.

The leading opponent of the Acts was Francis Place, a London master tailor. He and Joseph Hume, a radical MP, persuaded the House of Commons to set up a committee to inquire into the Combination Acts. The members of the committee were all opponents of the Acts, and so were all the witnesses they called before them. The committee recommended that the Acts should be repealed, and Parliament followed its advice. By the end of 1824 the Combination Acts had been repealed.

The result surprised everybody. Prices had begun to rise, and workers wanted more pay. They therefore took advantage of their new freedom, formed unions and began a series of strikes, which were sometimes backed up with threats and violence. The government appointed another committee, made up of different people, to consider what ought to be done. They recommended that men should still be allowed to belong to unions for the purpose of fixing hours of work and rates of pay, but that they should not be allowed to molest or threaten their employers or other workers. In 1825 Parliament passed an Act along these lines. Unions were now legal and could even ask their members to strike. But they could only sit and watch if some workers decided to ignore the strike call and went to work as usual.

The Grand National Consolidated Trades Union

For many years after the repeal of the Combination Acts, most unions were small local clubs with hardly any national organisation. These unions were often too weak to fight the employers. In 1834, for example, a large number of workmen went on strike in Derby, and their masters refused to take them back unless they promised never to join a union again. The Derby men asked for help, and clubs and societies all over the country promised to support them. Delegates from these clubs met and decided that trade unions needed a new nationwide organisation which would make sure that all the unions were working together and helping one another in the best possible

Robert Owen thought people ought to own everything they produced. He tried various schemes to put this into effect, but none of them worked

The Tolpuddle Martyrs

In 1833 in the Dorset village of Tolpuddle farmers were paying their labourers eight shillings a week. The labourers protested that this was too little. This annoyed the farmers who at once cut the rate to seven shillings, and threatened to reduce it to six in the near future. One of the labourers, George Loveless, a methodist preacher, heard of the Grand National Consolidated Trades Union and decided to organise a union branch for his fellow workers. The idea was that all the members would act together in bargaining with local farmers for better pay.

This was a serious business and, on joining, every member had to swear on the Bible not to tell anyone what was said at meetings. One of those who joined was gardener to a local magistrate. He told his master all about this oath. The magistrate was very alarmed, and got in touch with the Home Secretary, Lord Melbourne, who decided that the oath was illegal. In February 1834 Loveless and five of his fellow members were arrested and imprisoned in Dorchester jail. In March they were put on trial for adminstering an illegal oath. After the judge's summing up, which was very much against them, Loveless handed in a statement which read:

> My Lord, if we have violated any law, it was not done intentionally. We have injured no man's reputation, character, person or property. We were uniting together to preserve our selves, our wives and our children from utter degradation and starvation. We challenge any man, or number of men, to prove that we have acted or intended to act, different from the above statement.

Loveless and his companions were found guilty and sentenced to seven years' transportation. Melbourne was assured that the men were thoroughly bad characters and he confirmed the sentence. They were shipped off to Australia.

The Tolpuddle affair made a great stir. Many people felt that the labourers had been prosecuted and sentenced just to frighten other people off joining Owen's union. After all, the

way. They therefore founded the Grand National Consolidated Trades Union. They were encouraged by Robert Owen, the owner of the cotton mill at New Lanark. He believed that through this new union workers would be able to take control of the whole of industry, and eventually, perhaps, of the government of the country. Huge numbers of workers flocked to join the union. It soon claimed over 500,000 members, many of them unskilled labourers who had never joined a union before.

It was too good to last. The union was badly organised and, to make matters worse, many employers forced their workers to sign a 'document' promising not to join a union. The Grand National Consolidated began to lose members. It was further weakened by the punishment meted out to the Tolpuddle Martyrs and within a few months the union had collapsed.

law under which they had been sentenced was passed in wartime, and had only been intended to apply to the army and navy. Moreover, in spite of what Melbourne had been told, the men were all responsible and steady characters. Soon a Dorchester Committee was formed to work for the release of the labourers. A petition was circulated and was signed by 250,000 people. It was brought to London and a procession of 30,000 men took it to the House of Commons. Melbourne refused to look at it. The crowd dispersed. In time, the agitation died down and in 1836 the Toldpuddle Martyrs were pardoned, but it was forty years before another farm-workers' union was formed.

The beginnings of free trade

From 1823 onwards William Huskisson, the President of the Board of Trade, and Frederick Robinson, the Chancellor of the Exchequer, worked together to alter the system of taxation and help Britain's trade. Both men believed in free trade. They thought that every country ought to grow or manufacture those things which suited its climate and resources best, and buy any other goods it needed from other countries, paying for what it bought by selling some of its products. They believed that this system could work properly only if goods were allowed to pass freely from one country to another without any duties being paid, and they argued that

The procession escorting the Tolpuddle petition leaves Copenhagen Fields on the outskirts of London. According to some accounts 100,000 people were present

one of the reasons why Britain had slumps in trade was that there were so many customs duties on goods entering and leaving the country.

There were two reasons for these duties. Some of them were used to raise money for the government. Others had been imposed to protect British industries from foreign competition. Huskisson realised that he would have to leave duties which raised a lot of money for the government, but he decided he could safely cut those which were there to protect industry. In 1824 he cut duties on rum, raw silk and wool and allowed finished silk goods to be imported for the first time. In 1825 he cut the duties on most manufactured goods from 50 per cent to 20 per cent and reduced the duties on more raw materials. Huskisson also altered the Navigation Acts. These laid down that all imports to Britain had to be carried in British ships or in the ships of the country from which the goods came. After 1825 free entry to Britain's ports was allowed to the ships of any country which would do the same for Britain in return. This made trade with Britain cheaper and easier.

The sliding scale

Huskisson's work helped Britain's trade to expand, but he frightened many manufacturers, who feared that they might be put out of business by cheap foreign imports. But he only met really determined opposition when he tried to alter the Corn Law. Huskisson probably believed that there ought to be a free trade in corn, but farmers and landowners thought this would mean that they would get less for their crops. Huskisson was therefore only able to persuade the government to bring in a sliding scale. It worked this way. When British wheat was below fifty-two shillings a quarter, no foreign wheat could be imported. Once wheat reached that price, imports were allowed on payment of a duty of thirty-three shillings and eight pence a quarter. As the price rose, so the duty fell. When the British price reached seventy-three shillings the duty was only one shilling. At eighty shillings foreign wheat was admitted duty free. In practice the sliding scale

meant that little foreign wheat was imported until British prices reached sixty-five shillings, but the price of wheat continued to rise and fall, and bread was still expensive for working people to buy. Huskisson's work on free trade was only a beginning. Many duties still remained, but by the time he resigned in 1828 he had helped to reduce the cost of coffee, glass, books, paper, china, salt and many other everyday items. This cut the cost of living and helped to improve the standard of life of ordinary people.

Wellington's ministry

Early in 1827 the Tory Prime Minister, Lord Liverpool, had a stroke and retired from politics. He had been Prime Minister for fifteen years and it was difficult to find a replacement. Eventually Canning took over, but he was a sick man, and three months later he died. Frederick Robinson, now in the House of Lords with the title of Viscount Goderich, was persuaded to take over as Prime Minister. Unfortunately, although he understood finance, he found it very difficult to make up his mind about anything else. In particular he was unable to deal with the king, who bullied him unmercifully. It was said that Goderich sat weeping at Cabinet meetings, and he was described as 'firm as a bullrush'. In December 1827 he resigned and in January 1828 the Duke of Wellington became Prime Minister. He remained in office for two years, and had to spend most of his time dealing with the Irish problem.

Problems in Ireland

At the beginning of the nineteenth century the Irish had many grievances. The population was large and rising. In 1800 it had stood at about 5 million. By 1828 it was about 7½ million. There were very few industries in Ireland. Most of the inhabitants made their living by farming. Because the population was so large, there was a shortage of land and each family had only a small plot on which to grow its food. They grew a small amount of grain which was sold for cash to pay the rent. Their main crop was the potato, the only one which did well enough in Ireland's damp climate to supply food for all. Most people were wretchedly poor, but because land was scarce, rents were high. Most of a family's income therefore went to pay the landlord. To make matters worse, the majority of the landowners lived in England. Thus much of the wealth that Ireland produced was spent in England, benefiting English trade and industry while the Irish grew steadily poorer.

The Irish also felt that their religion was badly treated. Though most of the landowners were Protestants, the vast majority of the people were Catholics. Yet they had to pay tithes (a form of tax) which went to the Protestant Church. What was more, though some Catholics had the vote, only Protestants were allowed to hold any public office or become MPs.

Many Irishmen felt very bitter. In 1798, dur-ing the war against France, there had actually been a rebellion in Ireland against British rule, but it had easily been crushed. To try to make sure that this could not happen again, the government had decided to do away with the Irish Parliament, and thus bring Ireland under more direct British control. It was difficult to per-suade the Irish to agree to this, and in the end the government had promised that in return they would give Catholics equal rights. In 1800 the Act of Union was passed but George III had refused to allow his government to give Catholics equal rights.

Catholic Emancipation

The Irish were very angry at the government's refusal to 'emancipate' the Catholics—or, in other words, to give them the same rights as everyone else. In 1823 their leader, Daniel

The doctor, Wellington, helped by his assistant, Peel, is forcing the medicine of Catholic Emancipation down the throat of his unwilling patient, John Bull, who complains it will upset his constitution

O'Connell, set up the Catholic Association, whose main aim was to win political rights for Roman Catholics. At first it cost just over a pound a year to join, but in 1824 the rules were changed to allow anyone to become a member for a penny a month. The pennies flowed in, and by 1825 the association had an income of £1,000 a week.

The Catholic Association was now very powerful and had plenty of money, some of which was spent in putting up candidates for Parliament. In 1828 there was a by-election in County Clare, and O'Connell himself stood for election. Everybody knew that, as he was a Roman Catholic, he would not be allowed to take his seat in Parliament. But in spite of this he was elected.

Wellington was now faced with a very difficult choice. On the one hand he knew that the king, the vast majority of the Tory party and probably most Englishmen were opposed to Catholic Emancipation. They had been brought up to hate and fear the Roman Catholic Church. On the other hand, Wellington understood Irish politics. Twenty years earlier he had been Chief Secretary for Ireland and he now feared that if he refused to allow O'Connell to sit in the Commons, the whole of Ireland might explode into rebellion. He was not prepared to take the risk, and he set to work to persuade the rest of his party that they would have to grant Catholic Emancipation. After a long struggle he succeeded, and in 1829 Parliament passed the Catholic Relief Act which allowed Roman Catholics to occupy any public office except those of Lord Chancellor and Viceroy of Ireland. But this was not quite the end of the story. At the same time, an Act was passed which altered the qualification to vote in Irish elections. Previously, freeholders owning land with a rateable value of forty shillings (£2) a year had been allowed to vote. In 1829 the amount was raised to £10. This meant that many Catholics lost the vote. Finally the Catholic Association was disbanded, and because O'Connell's election for County Clare had taken place before the Act had been passed, he was made to stand for re-election before being allowed to take his seat.

The grant of Catholic Emancipation had important results. Wellington split his party. Many Tories refused to support a man who they thought had betrayed his country's religion, while the Irish learned that the threat of force will sometimes succeed where reason has failed.

3 A Changing Society

By 1830 the Tory government had reformed the police, the prisons, the system of taxation and the treatment of Catholics. Most MPs hoped that no further changes would be needed. But society was changing much faster than many of them realised and they soon had new problems to solve.

The rising population

Year	England & Wales	Scotland	Ireland	Total
1811	9.5	1.8	6 (est)	17.3
1821	12	2.1	6.8	20.9
1831	13.9	2.4	7.7	24
1841	15.9	2.6	8.2	26.7
1851	17.9	2.9	6.5	27.3

The increase in population between 1815 and 1851 (in millions)

Between 1811 and 1851, the number of people in Britian was rising. As the table shows, the total population of the British Isles rose by 10 million—from almost 17½ million in 1811 to almost 27½ million in 1851. In England, Wales and Scotland the increase was steady. In Ireland the population reached a peak of over 8 million just before the famine, and then fell back to 6 million in 1851. The biggest increase was in towns. In 1800 London was the only town in Britain with more than 100,000 inhabitants. In 1851 there were nine. Nearly half the town-dwellers had been born in the country, and had moved to the town in search of work in factories and mills. In 1851, for the first time, the majority of people lived in towns rather than villages. Britain had become an industrial nation.

It is very difficult to be certain why the population rose so rapidly. Historians agree that it must have been due to an increase in the birth-rate, a decrease in the death-rate, or both. Some maintain that the death-rate was going down, especially among young children. They point out for instance that the number of deaths from smallpox, a very dangerous and highly infectious disease, was falling fast. This was partly because many children were being vaccinated against smallpox and partly because the germ which caused the disease was becoming weaker. Some historians also argue that lives were saved because doctors were more skilled, there were more hospitals, and new brick houses were healthier than old timber and plaster dwellings. In addition, farmers were growing more vegetables so that people's diet was better and more varied. Factory-made cotton clothes were lighter and easier to wash than heavy wool and linen which most people used to wear. Thus the population was cleaner and healthier, and fewer young children died. Those who survived lived longer, and the population rose.

Other historians disagree. They agree that deaths from smallpox were declining but point out that other diseases, like cholera, were killing people off in the new industrial towns where living conditions were very unhealthy. They also argue that hospitals were so badly run and unhealthy that they probably increased the death-rate, and that so few people consulted doctors that it made no real difference how skilled they were. They say that the main reason for the increasing population was that people in or near factory towns were marrying earlier and having more children. A young man could easily marry and bring up a family on his wages in a cloth mill. What was more, he knew that in a few years he would be able to send his children out to work and thus bring even more money into the home. This meant that the birth-rate rose, and, with the death-rate steady or falling slightly, the population went up.

Unfortunately there is no certain way of telling which of these views is correct. There are no reliable figures for births and deaths in Britain until 1837, when registration was made compulsory. It may well be that both sides are right—that the death-rate was falling, and the birth-rate was rising.

Coping with a rising population

The rise in Britain's population had important effects on the country's history. In the first place, it meant that more food was needed. This encouraged the country's farmers to increase their production by improving crops and animals and by draining and ploughing more land. They knew that they could sell all they could grow (see Chapter 4). By 1851, however, it was clear that Britain could no longer be sure of producing enough to feed all her people. Food had to be imported in larger and larger

quantities. The growing population had to be housed. Most of them found homes in new industrial towns. They also had to be clothed, and their houses had to be furnished. All this provided work for the mills and factories where so many of them earned their living. The factories with their power-driven machinery were able to produce more goods than Britain needed. They sold the surplus overseas to pay for the food which had to be imported.

The domestic system

During the eighteenth century great changes took place in British industry. In 1700 the most important industry in England was making woollen cloth. In Scotland it was making linen. The spinning-wheels and looms which were used to make cloth were small and could easily be worked by a man or woman in their own home. In some houses a special workshop was built for the looms, but the spinning-wheel often stood in a corner of the living-room. At regular intervals a man called to bring supplies of raw material and take away finished pieces. Most cloth workers were helped by their wives and families and at busy times they often

The New Lanark Mills, built by David Dale, were made famous by Robert Owen, who took a great interest in his workers' welfare. Some of them thought he interfered too much

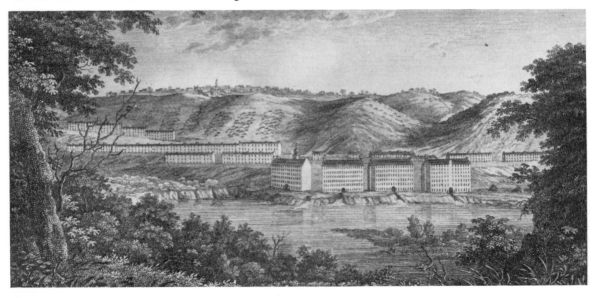

Early spinning-jennies were small enough to be worked by hand. Those used in factories were much larger, with many more spindles

worked cruelly long hours. Mary Thorpe, who lived at Bulwell in Nottinghamshire, described how small children were sometimes kept up by their parents till midnight stitching gloves. According to her, mothers used to 'pin them to their knee to keep them to their work and give them a slap to keep them awake'. But when work was slack there was time to cultivate their gardens, grow a little food, and enjoy some leisure.

The new factories

The changes began when merchants started to import large amounts of cheap cotton from India. This cotton had to be spun into thread and woven into cloth, and there was too much of it for the spinners and weavers to deal with. People racked their brains to find some method of speeding up spinning and weaving. In 1733 Kay invented the flying shuttle, which speeded up weaving, and in 1767 Hargreaves patented his spinning-jenny, which would spin eight threads at once. By 1790, two outstandingly successful spinning-machines had been invented. One, the water frame, was patented by Richard Arkwright. The other, the mule, was invented by Samuel Crompton. These new machines could spin up to a hundred fine even threads at a time. No one using a spinning-wheel could compete with them. The frame and the mule were too large, too complicated and too expensive to be used in the home. Instead they were housed in factories, and for the first time cloth workers had to go out to work. The machinery in early factories was driven by a water-wheel, which needed a steady flow of water to keep it turning. This meant that factories had to be built by the side of streams or rivers, and if a manufacturer found a good run of water in a deserted valley, he built his factory there, moved the machines into it, and brought workers from miles away. To house the workers he would, if necessary, build a whole new village. All this was very expensive, but provided the machinery was kept working twelve hours a day, the manufacturer could easily make a profit.

Early steam-engines were clumsy and unreliable, but by 1820 they were reliable enough to replace water wheels as the source of power for mills

Factory villages

Towards the end of the eighteenth century many manufacturing villages were built. They were usually fairly small, and were often miles from the nearest large town. Examples in Scotland are New Lanark, Stanley and Deanston, each of which was built round a water-powered cloth mill. Often there were no roads near sites of new factories, and manufacturers had to have roads built so that they could bring in raw material and take away finished goods. These roads benefited other people living nearby. Local farmers and tradesmen were also pleased by the arrival of the spinners, mill-wrights, carters, clerks and other tradesmen who were

needed to keep the factory working. All of them had to be fed, and many earned good money, much of which found its way into the pockets of the locals. Often the gentry were not so pleased. They feared that factory workers might misbehave. Usually, however, factory owners kept a sharp eye on their workers, even during the time they were not at work. Some took great care of them, setting up schools, libraries and hospitals. Many set up shops where their workers could buy all the provisions they needed. This was a mixed blessing, however. In some cases the owners would not allow any other shop to open in the village, and charged very high prices for what they sold. A few went even further, and instead of paying their workers in cash, gave them tokens which had to be exchanged for goods in the company shop. This system, which was known as 'truck', was very unpopular with workers and in 1831 it was made illegal.

The growth of towns

Before the end of the eighteenth century all the best waterside sites had been used. Indeed, on some rivers there were so many mills that there was not enough water to drive them all. Fortunately, thanks to James Watt, there were now steam-engines which were reliable enough to power factories. With the coming of the steam-engine, mills no longer had to be built on the riverside. Instead, factory owners chose sites that were close to existing towns, where roads were better, and where there were plenty of people to man the machines. As the number of

factories increased, workers flocked to the towns. Some of them came from the countryside where the population was rising fast, others came from Ireland or, in Scotland, from the Highlands. So towns steadily grew larger.

Working conditions

The growth of factories and of large industrial towns caused problems which eventually had to be tackled by the government. In the first place factories could be unhealthy and dangerous. New large mills were show-pieces attracting large numbers of sightseers who found much to admire. At Deanston Cotton Mill in Perthshire, for instance, the apartments were 'clean, well ventilated' and had the machinery 'well fenced'. There were changing rooms for the workers with piped water laid on. As a result, the workers were a 'cheerful, happy-

By the beginning of the nineteenth century the spinning machines invented by Arkwright and Crompton had been improved and enlarged. This engraving shows rows of machines in a nineteenth-century factory

looking set of industrious men and women'. Many smaller, older mills were very different. They were stuffy and cramped. Spinning-machines with whirling shafts driven by huge leather belts were packed so closely together that there was hardly room to pass between them. The machines were not fenced off and accidents were common. One foreman recalled how he had seen a girl's clothing caught round a shaft which twisted her round and eventually tore her clothes off completely. She was lucky. Some workers had their hands or arms torn off, while a few were killed.

Others had their health ruined. In some cotton-spinning factories the air round the machines was filled with tiny fragments of cotton, which the workers breathed in. After a while they became hoarse, and developed a persistent cough. In linen-spinning factories conditions were much worse. To keep the flax from sticking together, it was spun in a continuous spray of water, which drenched the girls who worked at the machines. A girl employed by Mill, Cruden & Co. in Aberdeen complained that she was 'wet through and through', that she had constant coughs and colds, and could rarely sleep because her throat was so sore. Her legs and feet were so swollen she could hardly walk, and she was getting very deaf. It was, she said, 'a shame to set people to such work'.

By today's standards hours of work in factories were very long. In 1833 Woodside Cotton Mill in Aberdeen was at work from 6 a.m. until 8 p.m., with two breaks of forty-eight minutes each for breakfast and dinner. What was more, the workers usually had to spend about twenty minutes of their dinner hour cleaning the machinery. Such hours were quite common. Indeed, if factories were really busy, they would stay open for as long as sixteen or eighteen hours a day.

As a rule, most members of Parliament thought that conditions of work were none of their business. They thought that it was up to employers and workmen to bargain with one another and agree how many hours they should work and what the rates of pay should be. The trouble was that many factory workers were

children. Most of them were piecers who had to watch the spinning-machines and, if a thread broke, join the two ends together again. This job required no strength, but it needed a sharp eye and nimble fingers. It was thus ideal for children. Some were very young—five or six—but most mills would not take on children younger than eight or ten. But, whatever their age, they were expected to stay at work all the time the mill was open.

The first Factory Acts

Most members of Parliament agreed that children had to be protected from the effects of the factory system. Some wanted to go further. They believed that hours of work for adults as well as children should be limited by law, and wanted Parliament to pass an Act reducing the hours of work to ten a day. In most manufacturing towns there was a 'Ten Hours Committee', and several MPs, including Michael Sadler and John Fielden, were in favour of a 'Ten Hours Act'. Parliament refused to go as far as this. Instead they passed several Acts which, by 1832, limited the hours of work in cloth mills for all those under eighteen to twelve hours a day. In fact, so many of the workers were children that this meant that factories ought to have closed after twelve hours. But nobody was appointed to make sure that the law was enforced, so many factory owners continued to run their mills for up to sixteen hours a day at busy times.

Life in the towns

Throughout the first half of the nineteenth century industry continued to expand. So did towns. The population of Manchester increased from about 40,000 in 1785 to 142,000 in 1831, while that of Glasgow went up from 77,000 in 1801 to 345,000 in 1851. All these extra people had to have somewhere to live, and huge numbers of houses were built to accommodate them. As a rule, landowners packed as many houses as they could onto their land, because the more houses they had, the more rent came in. They wasted no money, and

Tumbledown lodging houses in the London slums. The narrow street is crowded with traders' stalls, people and animals—including a pig

refused to provide pavements, piped water, sewers, street lights, shops or schools. Streets were laid out without any overall plan, so that new industrial towns were vast sprawling masses of houses and factories. 'Manchester and Salford,' wrote a surgeon in 1840, 'with a population of probably 260,000 souls, is a huge overgrown village, built according to no definite plan.'

In most towns houses were grouped round a court, often with a pump in the middle. This was usually the only water supply. There were no sewers. The sewage was allowed to accumulate in cesspits, which were emptied from time to time. Such places were bound to be unhealthy, but they were made much worse by overcrowding, as more people flooded into towns in search of work. In 1839 it was reckoned that about 8,000 cellars in Liverpool were shared by 39,000 people, while in Bury about a third of the working population slept three or more to a bed. The worst conditions were in common lodging houses, where newcomers often had to stay while they looked for a permanent home. The town clerk of Morpeth in Northumberland wrote that beds in such places were

> filled with as many as can possibly lie on them. Others find berths below the beds, and then the vacant places on the floor are occupied. Among these is a tub filled with vomit and natural evacuations.

Some lodging houses had no beds at all, and men, women and children were packed side by side on the floor 'so as not to leave sufficient space upon which to set a foot'. A London clergyman noticed that lodging houses were 'never cleaned or ventilated', so that it was 'almost impossible to breathe'. They swarmed with bugs and lice of all kinds. 'I have felt the vermin dropping on my hat like peas,' he said.

Foreign visitors were horrified by Britain's industrial towns. A French lawyer named de Tocqueville visited Manchester in 1835. He wrote that 'a sort of black smoke' covered the city, which was filled with the noise of 'the crunching wheels of machinery, the shriek of steam from boilers, the regular beat of the looms' and 'the heavy rumble of carts'. He saw 'heaps of dung, rubble from buildings, putrid, stagnant pools . . . roads full of ruts and puddles . . . lined with one-story houses with ill-fitting planks and broken windows'. A French writer named Taine went to Liverpool where he found

> fifteen or twenty streets with ropes stretched across them where rags and underwear were hung out to dry. Every stairway swarms with children, five or six to a step. Their faces are pale, their hair whitish and tousled, the rags they wear are full of holes, they have neither shoes nor stockings and they are all vilely dirty. Their faces and limbs seem to be encrusted with dust and soot.

Taine looked into some of the rooms: 'A threadbare slip of oilcloth on the floor, the children tumble over each other. The smell is that of an old-clothes shop full of rotting rags.'

People who lived in these slums often tried to escape from their misery by drinking. There were plenty of beer shops. An Act of Parliament passed in 1830 allowed anyone to sell beer on payment of a fee of just over £2 and in 1848 it was reckoned that there were 11,000 shops selling drink in London alone. Most of them sold beer at three pence a quart. This was very cheap and to make a profit they had to water the beer down and add various chemicals, some of them poisonous, to make it look and taste as strong as before. This had a terrible effect on drinkers, who were slowly poisoned by the combination of alcohol and the chemicals added by shopkeepers.

Towns and public health

It was difficult for labourers in towns like Manchester, Glasgow or Birmingham to live healthy lives. They worked long hours in stuffy, overcrowded factories and, even outside the works, the air they breathed was polluted with fumes and smoke. Their homes were likely to be overcrowded and damp. The water they drank was probably infected and much of their food contained poisonous chemicals. Many were constantly ill with stomach upsets, sore throats and bad chests. It is no wonder that they tended to have shorter lives than those who lived in the country. Labourers in the farming county of Rutland could expect to live more than twice as long as those in Manchester.

The situation was made worse in 1832, when cholera appeared in Britain for the first time and swept across the country, killing thousands of people. It is a horrible disease, causing a high fever, cramping stomach pains, sickness and constant diarrhoea. Death is caused by dehydration—the victims lose so much liquid that they shrivel up. The whole country was affected by cholera, but large towns suffered most. We know now that cholera is caused by infected drinking water, but in the middle of the nineteenth century nobody knew this for certain. Many people took it for granted, however, that the disease was connected with 'insanitary' living conditions, and in 1839 the House of Lords asked Edwin Chadwick to prepare a report on the sanitary condition of the labouring population of Great Britain.

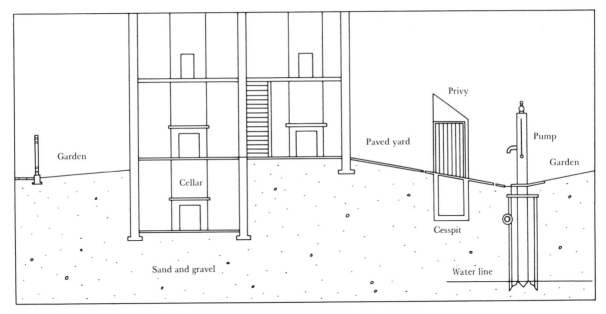

This diagram, copied from a Royal Commission report of 1843, shows how a leaking cesspit could pollute the water supply

By 1839 Chadwick had already done much important work. He had drawn up the 1833 Factory Act, and as Secretary of the Poor Law Commissioners, was mainly responsible for the 1834 Poor Law (see Chapter 6). His report for the House of Lords was compiled from information he got from Poor Law Boards all over the country, and it gave the first nationwide picture of how the poor lived. It was a horrifying report, but little was done until 1848 when there was another outbreak of cholera and Parliament passed a Public Health Act. This set up a Board of Health, whose members included both Lord Ashley and Chadwick.

The board members worked hard. They tried to make sure that every town had a proper water supply, good sewers and enough space set aside for burying the dead. But they had no power to force local councils to follow their advice. What was more, Chadwick had no tact, and upset many officials. As a result, the board achieved very little and was disbanded in 1854.

It was another twenty or thirty years before anything effective was done to clean up the slums in Britain's industrial towns.

Factory owners and managers lived in the same towns as the workers, but they built themselves large houses as far as possible from the slums. Usually their homes were at the west end of the town, to avoid the factory smoke and smells carried on the prevailing westerly winds. Taine noticed that the richer streets had no shops, but consisted of rows of houses with 'well-mowed lawns, little iron gates, all of it fresh and neat'. These houses were often crammed with furniture and ornaments. There were servants to dust and clean, prepare meals, do the washing, light fires and fetch and carry. In such houses the owner was 'king of his family and servants' and able to relax in comfort after his day's work. As a rule he travelled to and from his work in a horse-drawn cab, but by 1850 a few factory owners lived many miles from their works and travelled by train.

4 Life in the Countryside

At the beginning of the nineteenth century British farmers could afford to feel pleased. They had managed to increase food production steadily throughout the eighteenth century so that by 1800 the country was producing double the amount of food that had been grown in 1700. This was just as well because during the same period the population too had nearly doubled, from just over 9 million to about 16 million. If the farmers had not increased their

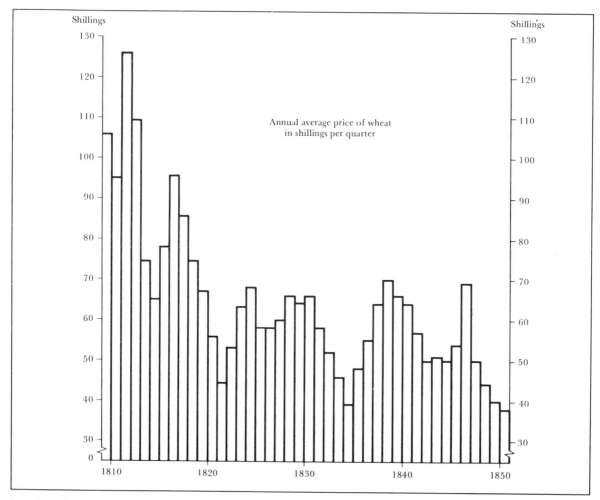

Annual average price of wheat in shillings per quarter

It is clear from this bar chart that neither the sliding scale nor the repeal of the Corn Law had much effect on the price of wheat

production, many people would have gone hungry. Changes in the system of farming were thus of vital importance to the whole country.

The open-field system

At the beginning of the eighteenth century farming in large areas of Britain was still carried on much as it had been for hundreds of years. Many English villages still had their cultivated land lying in three huge open fields. These were split up into a very large number of narrow strips and every farmer in the village worked strips in each field. Only two of the fields were cultivated at a time. Every year one field was left lying fallow without any crop. This was to prevent it from losing its fertility. Around the village, apart from the open fields, there was a large area of common pasture on which each farmer had the right to graze a number of animals. The more strips he owned, the more animals he could graze.

Farmers in Scotland at this time used a rather different system. North of the border the land was divided into infield, outfield and pasture. The infield, which was the richest land, was cultivated all the time. The outfield was poorer land. Only a little of it was cultivated at a time; a crop was grown every year until the soil was exhausted. Once this had happened this part was put back to pasture and a different area was ploughed up and sown. As in England, the land was ploughed in long narrow strips and only the poorest soil was set aside for use as permanent pasture.

Today these old systems of farming seem very inefficient. Farm animals were particularly badly off. All the crops grown on the arable land were for human consumption, and as a result the animals had to live on what they could find on the pasture, supplemented by a little hay and straw in winter. Many had to be killed off in the autumn, and those that survived the winter were weak and under sized.

The disadvantages of the old systems of farming became more and more obvious as the population grew and the demand for food increased. Various suggestions were put forward to make farming more efficient and

increase food production. The most important of these suggestions was that special crops should be grown to feed the animals. For instance, some farmers found that if they sowed special seed, they grew a better crop of grass on their pasture. Others discovered that a crop of turnips could keep a large number of animals fit and well through the winter. These animals then produced more dung which could be used to increase the fertility of all the farm land and improve the quality of the crops. Other discoveries were also made. Farmers on acid soils found that they could grow better crops after they had dressed their land with lime, while others discovered that they could gradually improve the quality of their stock by using only their best animals for breeding.

As the eighteenth century went on, these ideas spread, and more and more farmers tried them out. Strips of turnips began to appear here and there scattered about the open fields. But it was not easy for a farmer to make big changes as long as his strips of land lay scattered about. In many villages farmers therefore tried to build up compact blocks of land by exchanging strips with other farmers who held land next to theirs. Slowly, small enclosed blocks of land began to appear among the narrow strips. But even this was second best. Efficient farmers really wanted all their land, including their share of pastures, enclosed together in one unit.

Enclosures

In Scotland it was not difficult to enclose the open fields. On most estates all the land was owned by one man who rented it out to the tenant farmers who worked it. Usually the lease was short and the landowner had the power, once the lease was up, to turn his tenants off and enclose the infield, outfield and pasture into a number of self-contained farms. In England it was not so easy. In most English villages a number of people owned the land and many more had grazing rights which were protected by law. In order to disentangle all this and redistribute the land in compact units it was necessary first to get a special Act of Parliament

Using a flail to thresh corn was hard and tedious work

passed. The whole process took much longer and was much more expensive than it was in Scotland. But it still seemed worthwhile, especially when grain prices were high.

In the eighteenth and early nineteenth centuries, grain prices varied a lot. The demand for food grew steadily as the population increased but the supply varied from year to year according to the weather. Farmers made most money when the crop was poor because when wheat was scarce, they got a much higher price for it. Wheat prices were at their peak between 1793 and 1815. Farmers therefore had plenty of money to spend on enclosures, and in this period alone about 2,000 Enclosure Acts were passed. This meant that by 1815 the majority of the old open-field villages had been enclosed.

Enclosures had an enormous effect on farming and on country life. In the first place, the amount of land available for cultivation greatly increased. By using one of the new crop rotations (see the diagram on page 38) a farmer could cultivate all his arable land instead of leaving a third of it lying fallow. In addition, about a million hectares of common pasture had been divided up between individual farms to be used as the owners thought best. In some places they ploughed up the old pasture and used it for crops. In others they put parts of old open fields down to pasture.

The new system was much more flexible than the old had been. It was now a simple matter to try out new crop rotations. Moreover, now that each farm had its own share of fenced pasture, it was easier to take proper care of the animals and select only the best for breeding. So the quality and quantity of both crops and livestock increased on enclosed farms. As a result, an enclosed farm was more valuable than one whose land still lay in strips in open fields, and farmers who wanted to buy or rent them had to pay more money.

Farming in 1815

In some ways, farming was much more skilled in 1815 than it had been a hundred years earlier. In the past most farmers had followed the same pattern of work and crops on the open fields, and this pattern had not varied much from year to year. Now farmers whose land had been enclosed were on their own, with a much wider choice of crops and methods than ever before. There were also new machines available. Two of these, the seed-drill and the horse-hoe, had first appeared as early as 1730. The seed-drill sowed seeds in straight lines instead of scattering them all over the surface of the ground as the old system of sowing by hand had done. Once the plants had come up in their neat straight lines, the farmer could use a horse-hoe to destroy the weeds growing between the rows and to keep the surface of the soil loose. But, even in 1815, these machines were not widely used. There were two reasons for this. In the first place, they worked best on light, sandy soils. Farmers on heavy land found that the soil stuck and clogged in them and soon gave up using them. Perhaps even more important, there were few people who knew how to make or repair machines like the seed-drill. It cost a lot to transport machinery over long distances, so that if there was not a local craftsman who could build and repair hoes and drills, it was cheaper to do without. Existing equipment like ploughs and wagons was improved but the only new machine whose use spread quickly was the threshing-machine, which separated the grain from the straw. This had been invented in 1786 by the Scotsman Andrew Meikle, and by 1815 it was common in all the corn-growing areas of the country—particularly the south and east. It was an efficient machine which enabled farmers to thresh corn with very little labour. It thus reduced the amount of work for labourers in winter, which was in any case a slack time. This made it unpopular with labourers.

To sum up, in 1815 some British farmers were still working old open-field systems, but most of them had enclosed farms and were using one of the new crop rotations. They grew turnips, clover and rye grass to feed their animals as well as grain crops to feed themselves. They used the animal dung to increase the fertility of the soil and this increased their crops. For nearly twenty years food prices had been rising faster than wages, rates or taxes. So farmers had become steadily richer.

After 1815, the process continued. To begin with, the farmers were protected from foreign competition by the Corn Law (see Chapter 1). Even when this was repealed in 1846 (see Chapter 8) most of them were still very well off. There were several reasons for this. Wheat prices remained high enough for farmers in good districts to make a fair profit, while the prices of other farm products tended to rise as well. The growing population needed more meat, eggs and vegetables, and the expanding railway network (see Chapter 9) meant that farmers could get their produce quickly and cheaply to the towns where it was needed. There were also developments in farming methods. In particular, a new method of draining land by using tile drains was discovered, and in 1846 the government made special loans

A threshing machine, usually powered by a horse-gin, did the work quickly and easily

to farmers who wished to drain their land. This was particularly useful for farmers on heavy soils who now found that their land could be made much more productive. Thus the second half of the nineteenth century began well for Britain's farmers.

	Field 1	Field 2	Field 3	Field 4
Year 1	Turnips	Barley	Clover	Wheat
Year 2	Barley	Clover	Wheat	Turnips
Year 3	Clover	Wheat	Turnips	Barley
Year 4	Wheat	Turnips	Barley	Clover

The famous Norfolk rotation of crops, which provided food for man and beast without exhausting the soil

The farmers' way of life

The farmers' way of life changed a good deal in the early nineteenth century. In open-field villages farmhouses had been grouped together in the middle of the village and most labourers had lived with the farmer and his family. Now that farms were enclosed, many rich farmers either built themselves fine new houses in the middle of their compact new holdings or else improved their old ones. In either case, they lived in great comfort and did not want to share their houses with labourers, who had to go and live in separate cottages. In 1859 a French traveller visited the home of an English farmer who rented 250 hectares, and was 'astounded' by the 'cool and lofty drawing-room' with 'curtains held by gilt loops, two elegantly framed looking-glasses, chairs in good taste' and 'a conservatory full of flowers'. The farmer's wife, with her 'perfectly white' hands, 'admirable' figure and 'high spirits' had learned to ride horses and to play the piano. She talked well and was, in fact, 'a lady'.

Not all farmers were so prosperous. In the old days there had been a large number of 'small farmers' who cultivated a few hectares of land with the help of their families and a few extra hands at harvest time. They had just managed to make farming pay under the old system but had no money to spend on experimenting with new crops and special breeds of animals. This meant that eventually their crops and livestock were not as good as those of their rich neighbours and fetched less money in the markets. Many of them could see no future in running their own farms and gave up their land. So throughout the eighteenth century the number of small farmers had been decreasing. It used to be thought that the cost of enclosure forced many of them to give up farming, but we now know that there were just as many small farmers in villages with enclosed farms as in open-field settlements. There were still a large number of them left at the beginning of the nineteenth century, living in small houses and working hard to make a living for themselves and their families. The most successful of them concentrated on mixed farming, growing vegetables for sale in towns. Growing corn was a much riskier business and few small farmers could afford to risk losing money on any of their crops.

The labourers' life

Most farm labourers had a hard time in the early nineteenth century. William Cobbett reckoned they were worse off than in the days when they had lived with the farmer and his family, because they were not paid enough to provide themselves with proper food and lodging. Certainly, wage rates in some areas were very low. Cobbett travelled widely round the south of England and was horrified by what he found. In 1825 he asked a man who was hedging on the side of the road how much he got a day. 'He said one shilling and sixpence. If the man have full work,' Cobbett went on, 'the whole nine shillings does not purchase a gallon loaf each for a wife and three children and two gallon loaves* for himself—nothing for lodging, washing, clothing, candlelight or fuel.' Years later Sir James Caird described the diet of such a labourer.

After doing up his horses he takes breakfast, which is made of flour with a little butter, and

* In the south of England a gallon loaf weighed 8lb 11oz, or 3.95kg.

water from the tea kettle poured over. He takes with him to the field a piece of bread and, if he can afford it, cheese to eat at midday. He returns home in the afternoon to a few potatoes. The supper commonly consists of bread and water.

Even the bread was poor quality. 'Twas that heavy and doughy,' said one labourer, 'ee could pull long strings of it out of your mouth.' They called it 'growy bread'. Caird pointed out that men on such a diet were less vigorous and active than they ought to have been and therefore did their work badly.

Labourers' houses were wretched. Cobbett wrote,

> Look at these hovels made of mud and of straw; bits of glass or of old cast off windows, without frames or hinges frequently, but merely stuck in the mud wall. Enter them, and look at the bits of chairs or stools, the wretched boards tacked together to serve for a table, the floor of pebble, broken brick or the bare ground. Look at the thing called a bed and survey the rags on the backs of the wretched inhabitants.

Most cottages had no toilets of any kind. The people just 'went broadcast' in the fields, while the children would 'just go anywhere, but mostly along by the side wall of the house. Once a week somebody would take a shovel and a barrow and clean the leavings up.'

Labourers in the north of England were usually better off than those in the south. This was because northern cloth mills were competing with farmers for workers and driving up rates of pay. In the south, on the other hand, there was no large-scale industry. Once there had been a lot of small firms making cloth, but many had been forced to close by the competition of big mills in the north. So a southern labourer had no choice. If he wanted a job, it had to be in farming. The situation was made worse by the fact that in the south there were far more men looking for work than there were jobs. This put farmers in a very strong position. They knew that a man would take a job at very low pay rather than run the risk of being out of work altogether.

This wretched cottage was the home of a farm labourer working near Blandford in Dorset in 1846

39

Inside the cottage the crumbling walls, cracked ceilings and simple furniture give a good idea of the poverty in which the labourer and his family lived

The main reason why there were so many labourers in the south looking for work was that the population there was increasing, while the number of jobs available stood still. Few people at the time realised this. They thought that men were out of work because farmers were employing fewer hands. They believed that new enclosed farms needed less labour. Many writers therefore blamed enclosures for unemployment and low wages, and it is only in the last thirty years that historians have shown once and for all that this is not true. Enclosed farms growing crops like turnips needed just as much labour as they had in the days when the land lay in open fields, and there were as many people working on the land in 1831 as there had been in 1811.

The Game Laws

Labourers could not afford to buy meat to eat and were often tempted to add to their diet by poaching for pheasants, hares or rabbits. But all these animals were the property of the land-owners and were protected from poachers by various means. Under a law passed in 1816, poachers caught in the act could be transported to Australia for seven years. Game was often guarded by spring-guns which were bolted in place and fired by a trip-wire. Sometimes man-traps were set. If a man trod on one, it snapped shut on his leg. Cobbett noticed a sign in Kent which read: 'Paradise Place. Spring-guns and steel traps are set here.' Most land-owners also employed gamekeepers who patrolled the estate armed with loaded guns and pistols. Occasionally poachers and game-keepers met and fought. In 1822 two young labourers were hanged at Winchester. One of them had killed a gamekeeper. The other had shot at one without harming him. Poaching was a risky business. A folk song put it like this:

Come all you gallant poachers that ramble free
    from care,
That walk out on moonlight nights with dog and
    gun and snare,
The jolly hares and pheasants you have at your
    command,
Not thinking that your last career is in Van
    Dieman's land.*

* Van Dieman's land was the island south of Australia now known as Tasmania. Many convicts were transported there in the early nineteenth century.

This is a humane man-trap. Some had metal teeth which bit into the leg

The Swing riots

Labourers could not be sure of regular work. In the past, when they had lived with the farmers, they had usually been employed for a year at a time, but now they were taken on by the week, by the day or even by the hour. At busy times like harvest most of them would be employed, but at slack times many of them would be unable to get farm work. This was particularly true in winter. Once a fair number of labourers had been employed in the winter months threshing the autumn grain crops, but most large farmers now had threshing-machines, which did the job much more quickly. This meant that in corn-growing areas there were often months at a time when it was difficult to get farm work. Instead, the parish authorities set the men to work in gangs repairing the local roads. Labourers in the south of England were in a wretched state. They were badly paid, badly housed and half-starved. They had no self-respect and were often out of work. They had every reason to feel bitter, especially when they saw how their employers, the farmers, were trying to use the Corn Law of 1815 to keep the price of bread artificially high.

As a rule labourers felt trapped and helpless, but in 1830, after a poor harvest and with grain prices high, they took the law into their own hands. There was a series of riots which amazed and frightened farmers and landown-ers. The trouble started in Kent in August and spread rapidly north and west. Everywhere the pattern was the same. Threatening letters, sometimes signed by a 'Captain Swing', were sent to farmers ordering them to smash their threshing-machines and increase labourers' pay. Then, one night, a gang of labourers would visit the farm. If the threshing-machine was still there, they would smash it to pieces, and would make the farmer pay a fine of bet-ween five shillings and £2. If the farmer prom-ised to increase his labourers' wages they would leave peacefully. Otherwise they might threaten to fire his haystacks. Many farmers argued that they could not afford to pay more but in the end they gave way. Some of them sympathised with the men's demands but in any case they realised that the labourers meant what they said.

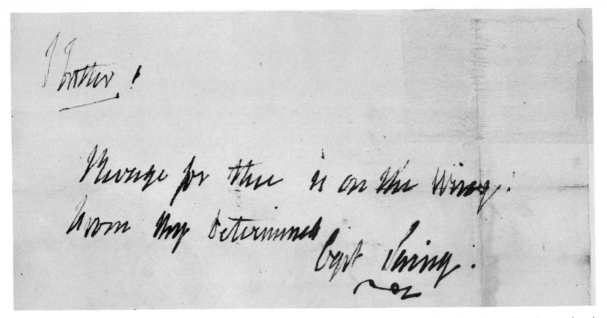

One of the letters sent by the Swing rioters. It reads: 'Revenge for thee is on the wing from thy determined Captain Swing'

The authorities feared that the Swing riots might be the work of a highly organised band of revolutionaries and some of them even believed that Captain Swing was a real person. In fact, there was no central organisation. Labourers in one village heard that riots in neighbouring places had helped to get a pay rise and decided that they might as well follow their neighbours' example. In some places there was little or no violence. In others, haystacks and even farmhouses were burned down. In all, fourteen counties were badly affected by the Swing riots. The local magistrates dealt with them in different ways. In Norfolk and Suffolk they issued a statement supporting the rioters. In other places they called out the yeomanry to arrest them. In the end about 2,000 men were put on trial for rioting, machine-breaking and stack-burning. Of these, 800 were acquitted, 500 were transported, nineteen were hanged and the remainder were imprisoned.

The riots had important results. Many threshing-machines had been destroyed—more than a hundred in Kent alone. It was a long time before most farmers bothered to replace them. They were unwilling to spend as much as £100 on a machine which their labour-ers might smash. So for the time being labourers got back their winter work. And the farmers paid the increased wages they had promised—at any rate for a year or two. So labourers got more money. In spite of the number who had been hanged, transported and imprisoned, many of them felt it had been worthwhile. 'Ah,' said one old man years later, 'them there riots and burnings did the poor a terrible deal of good.'

Conclusion

Though most farmers did well in the early nineteenth century, their labourers had a hard life. It is true that conditions varied from one village to another and even from farm to farm. But everywhere the work was hard and the hours were long. At busy times in the summer labourers might be on the go from three in the morning till seven at night. By the time they gave up work most of them were bent and limping, broken by a lifetime of drudgery. And then all they could look forward to was a corner in their son's cottage, or else a bed in the workhouse.

5 The Reform Act of 1832

The old system of voting

Before 1832, the British House of Commons was elected by a complicated system which had grown up over many centuries. England, Wales, Scotland and Ireland all elected members to sit in the Commons, but the rules which decided how the seats should be distributed and who should have the vote varied from place to place. There were two kinds of MPs, those representing counties and others elected by certain towns or boroughs.

County members

In 1830 every English county except Yorkshire returned two members to Parliament. Yorkshire, the largest county, returned four. Irish

An engraving of the House of Commons during a debate. The Speaker sits under the royal coat of arms. Government supporters sit on his right, opposition members on his left

Six counties in the south-west of England returned more than a quarter of all MPs before 1832. In Cornwall many small villages had been given MPs because most of the county belonged to the crown and would therefore return members loyal and obedient to the king

counties also had two members each. Welsh and Scottish counties had only one. In all, 188 county members were elected to the House of Commons. Only male landowners had the right to vote for county members. In England and Wales the owners of land which, if rented out, could be expected to bring in forty shillings or more a year, had the vote. These men were known as forty-shilling freeholders. In the Middle Ages this had been a high figure and only rich men qualified, but prices and rents had risen so much that by 1830 owners of quite small pieces of land had a vote. In Scotland the system was different and only a few landowners had the vote, while in Ireland the Catholic Relief Act of 1829 had raised the minimum figure to £10 (see Chapter 2). The number of voters varied enormously from county to county. In Yorkshire more than 23,000 voted in 1807. On the other hand, there were only about twenty electors in the county of Bute in south-west Scotland.

Borough members

In addition to the county members, 465 MPs were elected to represent the nation's boroughs. These were towns or villages which had at one time or another been given the right to send members to Parliament. One borough, Weymouth and Melcombe Regis, sent four members. Another 195 English and two Irish boroughs sent two each, while five English, two Welsh, one Scottish and thirty-one Irish boroughs sent one each. Finally, ten groups of Welsh and fourteen groups of Scottish boroughs each returned one member.

In England, Wales and Scotland the list of parliamentary boroughs had been more or less unchanged for over a hundred years. This meant that by 1830 it was quite out of date. Some towns which used to be important had, for various reasons, become smaller. For instance, the Normans had built the city of Old Sarum in Wiltshire on top of a hill because it

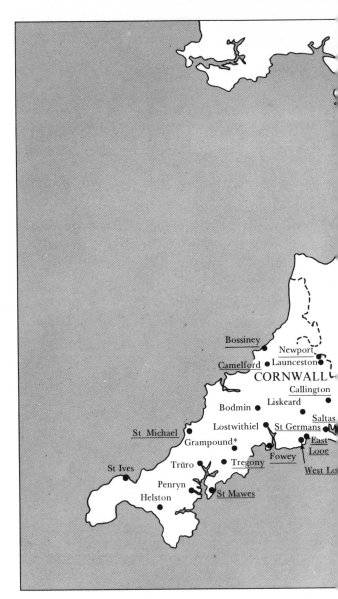

made it easy to defend. Once the country was at peace, the inhabitants left the hill top and went to live on the plains. By 1830 nobody lived in Old Sarum. But it still returned two members to Parliament. Almost all of the coastal borough of Dunwich in Suffolk had been washed into the sea. It, too, continued to return two MPs. On the other hand, since 1700 many large industrial towns had grown up. In 1831 Manchester was the centre of the cotton industry and Birmingham was famous for its engineering. Both had more than 100,000

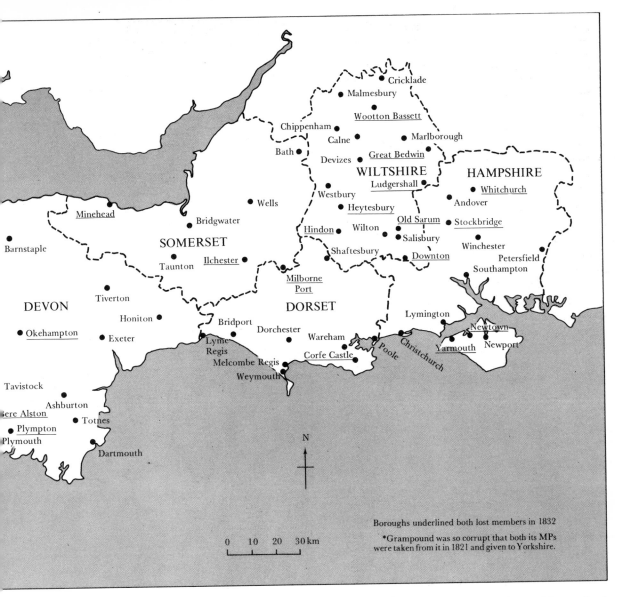

Boroughs underlined both lost members in 1832

*Grampound was so corrupt that both its MPs were taken from it in 1821 and given to Yorkshire.

inhabitants whose products were helping to make Britain rich. Yet neither town had any MPs. Merchants and manufacturers in places like Manchester and Birmingham thought it was high time their town was represented in Parliament instead of old, decayed places like Old Sarum.

The right to vote in boroughs varied from place to place. In some, most of the male inhabitants were voters. For instance, in 'pot-walloper' boroughs, every man who had a hearth on which he could boil a pot had the vote. Usually all the male residents had a hearth, so they all had a vote. Some potwalloper boroughs had more than 5,000 electors. In other boroughs all men who paid local rates known as 'scot and lot' had the vote. Westminster, a scot and lot borough, had over 16,000 electors. Many boroughs gave the right to vote to all those who had been granted or had inherited the freedom of the borough. In other towns, known as 'freehold' boroughs, all men who owned any land could vote. Some of these boroughs had more than 5,000 electors.

45

But in many boroughs only a very small proportion of the inhabitants had the right to vote. In some places, called 'burgage' boroughs, only the owners of certain pieces of land could vote. In such places there were rarely more than a hundred voters. Finally, in all Scottish burghs, most Irish and some English boroughs, only the council or corporation could vote. These were called 'corporation' boroughs. Many corporations were very small. Edinburgh had a population of well over 100,000, but the town council which elected the MP had only thirty-three members. To make matters worse, borough corporations were sometimes entirely under the control of a landowner. For instance, the corporation of Marlborough in Wiltshire consisted entirely of servants and tenants of the Marquis of Ailesbury. When it came to an election they paid no attention to the people of Marlborough, but always voted as the Marquis wished.

Pocket and rotten boroughs

A borough like Marlborough was said to be 'in the pocket' of the man who had the power to nominate its MPs. Such places were therefore called 'pocket' or 'nomination' boroughs. Some stayed under the control of the same families for many years. For example, the Eliot family nominated the MPs for St Germans in Cornwall at every election between 1660 and 1832. In other boroughs where there were only a few electors, they put their votes up for sale, and elected the man who offered the most money. One example is Gatton, a scot and lot borough in Surrey which consisted of six houses and had only six voters. The existence of such places meant that a man with plenty of money could always get himself a seat in Parliament. Many people disapproved of buying and selling votes. They thought it was corrupt, and described boroughs like Gatton as 'rotten' boroughs.

Elections

In many places, long before election time, the electors decided informally among themselves who should represent them in Parliament. Once this had happened there was no point in anyone else trying to get himself elected. So when the time came for the official election, the man they had chosen was the only candidate, and was returned unopposed. But if there was a large number of voters, several candidates would stand. Then every elector who wanted to take part had to go and declare his vote openly for all to hear. This system of 'open' voting made it easy for candidates to bribe or threaten electors, and many of them did. The hustings, where the votes were cast, consisted of a roofed platform with a few benches at one end. Hustings were also used by the candidates for making their most important speeches to the electors. There was only one hustings in each constituency.

Many electors lived a long way from the place where they were qualified to vote. For instance, at the beginning of the nineteenth century one of the Aberdeenshire voters lived at Margate in Kent. Such men had to spend a great deal of time and money travelling to and from the poll and they expected the candidate for whom they voted to pay all their expenses and entertain them free of charge. Even those who lived near the poll expected to be able to eat and drink for several days at the candidate's expense.

To cater for those who lived at a distance, the poll was kept open for as long as a fortnight. Since the voting was public it was easy to keep a check on how the poll was going. If, after a few days, one or two of the candidates were doing very badly, they might well withdraw. But if the contest was still close in the last couple of days, all the candidates would try their best to persuade the electors who had not yet voted to go and vote for them. In these circumstances they might easily offer £20 or more for a vote. So the electors would expect to do very well in a closely contested election.

Even those who did not have a vote looked forward to contested elections. They crowded round the hustings to listen to the speeches, cheering their favourites and jeering those they disliked. They also kept a close watch on the voting and would sometimes jostle and threaten electors who had voted for unpopular candidates. For this reason candidates tried to keep on good terms with all the local people. When one of the Duke of Northumberland's family stood for Westminster in 1806, the Duke sent his footmen to the city to distribute bread, cheese and beer to everybody. Francis Place, a leading radical, watched 'a dense crowd of vagabonds, catching the lumps, shouting, swearing, fighting'. They upset the barrels of beer in the street and then tried to scoop it up out of the gutters in their hats. All this was fine for the electors but it was very expensive for the politicians. The Yorkshire election of 1807 was reckoned to have cost all the candidates a total of £250,000. It was not surprising that politicians tried to avoid contested elections whenever they could.

Summing up

By today's standards there were many things wrong with the way in which Parliament was elected in 1832. It seems strange to us that so few people had the vote. In 1832 the total population of Britain, including Ireland, was about 24 million. It is impossible to know exactly how many of these had the vote because there were no registers, but the latest estimate is that the total was probably only about 420,000. Women could not vote. In the counties, men who rented all their property had no vote. They had to own at least some of it. The fact that there was no proper system to decide which places should send MPs to Parliament also seems ridiculous—a deserted place like Old Sarum sent two members to the Commons, while Manchester,

The hustings for a parliamentary election in Covent Garden, London. Not many people in this huge crowd could hear what the speaker was saying

47

a large, bustling and wealthy town, sent none. It is also difficult to understand today how people could put up with open voting and all the bribery and intimidation that played such an important part in early nineteenth-century elections.

Many people who lived at the time would have disagreed with these criticisms. Lord Braxfield, the Scottish judge, said that the British constitution was 'the best in the world', while in 1830 the Duke of Wellington, in a famous speech, spoke of the 'excellence' of the system, and said that he did not see how it 'could be improved or be rendered more satisfactory'. Such men argued that the system worked well. They pointed out that the House of Commons contained members representing all the most important 'interests' in the country. There were landowners, lawyers, soldiers, traders and manufacturers. With all these people in it, the House was bound to consider the wishes of the whole country when deciding its policies. It was true that the poor had no voice, but most politicians at this time believed that only those who owned property had any right to a say in how the country was run. In any case, the system had been very successful. Since 1700 the country had become steadily richer, and in 1815 it had just defeated Napoleon —something no other country had managed to do. It was very foolish to suggest that something so successful should be altered.

Other people were unhappy about certain aspects of Parliament. They did not approve of rotten and pocket boroughs, believing that seats ought to be taken from them and given to new industrial towns. They were, however, frightened that reform might lead to revolution. Rather than risk this they preferred to leave things as they were. Finally, there were the radicals who wanted to reform the whole system and replace it with one which would represent the wishes of the majority of the people.

The beginnings of reform

As time passed, the number of those who wanted to alter the system grew steadily. This was partly due to a great increase in the number of newspapers, which were distributed all over the country by the new speedy coach services. Previously people had only been aware of elections which took place in their own area. Now they were able to read about what was going on all over the country and many of them realised for the first time how corrupt the system was. Excursions to Old Sarum became quite popular. When Cobbett visited 'the Accursed Hill', he found himself 'swelling with indignation against the base and plundering and murderous sons of corruption'. As long as the country was prosperous and at peace, however, most people preferred to leave well alone. When trade was bad and disorder threatened, they were more likely to agree with Cobbett and call for Parliament to be reformed. Thus between 1815 and 1820, when trade was bad and prices were high, petitions in favour of reform had flooded into Parliament. But between 1824 and 1829 trade was good, prices were lower—and not a single reform petition had come in. Tories like Peel and Huskisson had worked on prison reform and free trade, while the Whigs spent most of their time fighting for Catholic Emancipation.

Wellington strongly opposed reform, but he was too wise to fight against it once he knew he would be beaten

48

By 1830, however, things were very different. The harvest was poor and food prices rose. People were therefore more restless and discontented than they had been for many years. The Catholic Relief Act of 1829 affected both main parties. A large number of Tories were so upset by it that they decided they would rather have a Whig government than a Tory government led by Wellington and Peel. On the other side of the fence, now that the Catholics had been given their rights, the Whigs began to argue in favour of the reform of Parliament. There was, they said, no longer any need to be afraid of change. Indeed, they argued that Catholic Emancipation, and the reforms which Huskisson and Peel had made in the tax system and the law, all showed that reasonable changes made in good time would never lead to violence. They might actually prevent it.

By 1830, therefore, there was much talk of altering the way in which MPs were elected, and reformers, inspired by the success of O'Connell's Catholic Association, established societies in various parts of the country to press for change. The most important, the Birmingham Political Union, was organised by Thomas Attwood. He got 15,000 to attend a public meeting in January 1830, and later presented a petition in favour of reform containing 30,000 signatures. Perhaps this interest might have died down in time, but just as it was reaching its peak, King George IV died and a general election had to be held. With the Tories split and reform so popular, the government lost a number of seats. Within a few weeks it was defeated on a vote in the House of Commons and the new king, William IV, called on the Whig leader, Lord Grey, to become Prime Minister. Grey did so, and at once set up a small committee to draft a Reform Bill.

How the Bill became law

Grey gave his committee a difficult job. It had to draw up a Bill which would satisfy public demands for reform without upsetting the whole system of government. The committee reckoned that the public would not be satisfied unless real and obvious changes were made. It

Lord Grey, who came from a family of Northumberland landowners, had been an MP since 1786. He had last been a government minister in 1807

therefore proposed that in future, voting qualifications in the boroughs should be the same all over the country; that some leaseholders, that is people who rented their land, should have the vote in counties; and, most important, that more than a hundred seats should be taken from the smallest boroughs and given to towns and counties with a large population. The committee's proposals were much more sweeping than most people had expected. So when Lord John Russell told the House of Commons what they had in mind, on 1 March 1831, MPs were astonished. 'They are mad, they are mad!' said one Whig member. He knew that the majority of the Commons would be against the Bill.

But, although the Bill was disliked in Parliament, it was very popular in the country. People were pleased that at last something worthwhile was to be done to reform Parliament, and demanded, 'The Bill, the whole Bill, and nothing but the Bill.' MPs began to change their minds, and when the Bill came up for its

Nottingham Castle burns, while an excited crowd cheers at the sight

second reading on 21 March, it was passed by one vote. This was good news, but there was still a long way to go; and on 20 April one of the clauses was defeated. Grey at once asked the king to dissolve Parliament, and at the election which followed his government was returned with a majority over the Tories of at least 130. The Bill was now certain to get through the Commons and on 22 September it was given its final reading by 345 votes to 246.

In order to become law, however, the Bill had to be approved by the House of Lords, where there was certain to be a majority against it. After a debate lasting five days, the Lords rejected it by a majority of forty-one. The result was an outbreak of rioting and disorder. The Duke of Wellington had his windows broken and a mob burned down Nottingham Castle, which was owned by the Duke of Newcastle, who had also voted against the Bill. Most of the

bishops had opposed reform, and as a result, many clergymen were hooted and pelted with stones and rubbish by angry crowds just because they were dressed like bishops.

But the most serious riots took place in Bristol at the end of October. They were caused by the visit of Sir Charles Wetherell, a leading opponent of the Bill. He had referred to borough householders as 'no better than paupers', and said that to visit them to ask for votes would be like going to a leper-house. This angered the citizens of Bristol, and to greet him they organised a huge demonstration which quickly got out of control. Soon the city was taken over by rioters. Many of them were young and most of them were drunk. They smashed their way into every public building they could find and set them all on fire. They broke into the Bishop's Palace, ransacked his wine cellar and sold his best wine in the street for a penny a bottle. Some collapsed unconscious in burning buildings and died. A troop of cavalry, less than a hundred strong, had been sent to keep order, but the officers did not at first dare to send the men against the great crowds of rioters.

After three days of rioting and looting, the mob began to tire. At last the cavalry charged and cleared the streets. The Customs House, the Excise Office, the Bishop's Palace, various jails and several toll houses had all been destroyed. There were also about 400 dead and injured.

The Bristol riots frightened the government. To make matters worse, bands of men up and down the country began to arm themselves in case rioting and looting broke out in their areas. Grey acted quickly. He recalled Parliament and introduced another Reform Bill. On 24 March 1832 it was passed by the Commons, and was sent up to the Lords, where there was still a majority against it. But two things had changed since October. The Bristol riots had made some of the Lords realise for the first time how many people supported the Bill, and how dangerous it might be to reject it. Also, the king promised that if the Lords voted against the Bill, he would create some new Whig peers to help get it through. So on 14 April the Lords reluctantly agreed to the Bill by 184 votes to 175. But they were still determined to alter it, and on 7 May they insisted, by 151 votes to 116, on making a change which Grey and his ministers would not accept. Grey therefore asked the king to create enough Whig peers to get the change reversed. William refused. He was prepared to create peers only if the whole Bill was in danger. Grey at once resigned. He was tired of struggling to get reform through Parliament.

From 9 May to 14 May Wellington tried to form a Tory government. In the meantime a meeting in favour of reform held in Birmingham was attended by 200,000 people. In London people queued up to withdraw their money from the Bank of England. Finally Wellington had to admit that he could not form a government and the king had to ask Grey to come back. He did so, but only on condition that William promised to create as many peers as were needed to get the Bill through the Lords unchanged. William gave way and the Whig government returned to office. Once the Tories knew that the king would support Grey, they realised that there was no point in voting against the Bill. So the Bill went through and became law on 4 June 1832.

Clauses of the Reform Acts

The main Reform Act applied only to England and Wales, but soon separate Acts were passed to deal with Scotland and Ireland. The 1832 Acts made important changes. First, fifty-six boroughs with populations of less than 2,000 lost the right to be represented in Parliament altogether, while thirty boroughs with between 2,000 and 4,000 inhabitants were allowed to keep only one member. This meant that there were now seats to spare. Sixty-five of these were given to the counties with the largest populations, and sixty-five to English and Welsh towns which had not been represented before. Eight extra seats were given to towns in Scotland and five extra to Ireland. This redistribution of seats still left great variations in the size of constituencies. For instance, the West Riding of Yorkshire, with 18,000 electors, and Rutland with 1,300, both returned two members, as did Westminster with 11,600 and Harwich with 214. But on the whole the situation was certainly much better than before.

So far as voting qualifications were concerned, the right to vote in the boroughs was given to the owners of all houses which could be rented out for £10 a year or more. In some industrial towns, where house prices were high, this meant that almost all male householders had a vote. In country towns it only applied to the owners of large houses. In the counties, the forty-shilling freeholders kept the vote, but it was also given to those who held land for which they paid £10 a year on a long lease, and those who held land worth £50 a year on a short lease. These reforms increased the total British electorate from about 400,000 to just over 800,000. The biggest increase was in Scotland, where the number of voters rose from about 4,500 to 65,000. But over the whole country still only about one in thirty of the population had the

	COUNTIES		BOROUGHS		UNIVERSITIES	
	1830	1832	1830	1832	1830	1832
England	1 × 4　　4 39 × 2　78	1 × 6　　6 26 × 4　104 7 × 3　21 6 × 2　12 1 × 1　1	2 × 4*　8 195 × 2　390 5 × 1　5	1 × 4*　4 133 × 2　266 54 × 1　54		
	_82_	_144_	_403_	_324_	4	4
Wales	12 × 1　12	3 × 2　6 9 × 1　9	2 × 1　2 10 groups　10	13 × 1　13		
	_12_	_15_	_12_	_13_		
Scotland	27 × 1　27 6 share　3	27 × 1　27 6 share　3	1 × 1　1 14 groups　14	2 × 2　4 5 × 1　5 14 groups　14		
	_30_	_30_	_15_	_23_		
Ireland	32 × 2　64	32 × 2　64	2 × 2　4 31 × 1　31	6 × 2　12 27 × 1　27		
	_64_	_64_	_35_	_39_	1	2
Totals	_188_	_253_	_465_	_399_	_5_	_6_

*Includes London

This table shows how the Reform Act changed the composition of the house of Commons (1 × 4 means one constituency returning four MPs and so on)

vote. Prosperous middle-class men could now vote, but hardly any working-class men had any say in how the country was run. Indeed, the fact that potwalloper and scot and lot boroughs had been abolished meant that fewer working men had the vote than before.

In fact the Reform Act did exactly what Grey had hoped. It satisfied most of those who had been calling for reform, but it did not destroy the old system. For the first time the House of Commons was elected according to a sensible set of rules which applied to the whole country. Most people accepted this and settled down to make the new system work. But it soon became obvious that in some ways not much had altered. For example, though it was no longer possible to buy and sell seats, there was still widespread bribery after 1832, because voting was still open. Landowners were still in charge. Some people had thought that once industrial towns got seats and middle-class people were given the vote, there would be a great increase in the number of tradesmen and industrialists in Parliament. This did not happen, mainly because people who had to work for their living could not afford the time to attend the Commons and keep the voters happy. Only landowners, living off their rents, could spare the time. There was one change, however. The new reformed Parliament was much more sure of itself than the old. As a result it set to work to reform many aspects of life in Britain.

6 The Whig Reforms, 1833–1835

The Reform Act of 1832 was only the first of several important reforms brought about between 1830 and 1835. The Whig Parliament also passed Acts to deal with education, slavery, the treatment of the poor and local government.

The grants to education, 1833

In 1830 there was no properly organised system of education in England and Wales. The rich could afford to send their children to private schools or to employ tutors to live with them. The poor had to rely on charity schools. These were controlled and paid for by various religious societies. The two biggest societies were the National Society, run by the Church of England, and the British and Foreign School Society, run by the non-conformists. These societies had set up schools all over the country. They tried to teach children to be good Christians, to work hard and to do as they were told. They taught reading, knitting and spinning or other 'coarse works as may fit them for servants'. Between 1800 and 1830 the population, particularly in towns, grew fast and the societies could not provide enough schools for all the children. In 1833 an inquiry showed that only about half the children were going to school. The government decided to help out and granted £10,000 each to the two biggest societies for building new schools. It was only a little, but each year the grant increased, and in 1839 a Privy Council Committee was set up to administer the money. It was the beginning of government control over education.

THE PATRON OF EDUCATION, AND FRIEND OF THE POOR.

In nineteenth-century schools much of the teaching was carried out by senior pupils who taught small groups of younger children their lessons

The abolition of slavery, 1833

Parliament spent a good deal of time in 1833 working on an Act to abolish slavery in British colonies. In 1771 Lord Mansfield, the Lord Chief Justice, had declared that slavery was illegal in England, and in 1807, after a long campaign, Parliament had made the slave trade illegal. This meant that British traders could no longer capture slaves in Africa and ship them across to the West Indies to be sold to the planters. It was, however, quite legal for sugar and cotton planters to own slaves. Some treated their slaves very badly. Government ministers made speeches warning them to be more humane. This had little effect. In 1833, therefore, Parliament passed an Act abolishing slavery in all British colonies. The freed slaves had to work for their former owners as apprentices for seven years, and £20 million was given to slave owners to compensate them—about £38 per slave.

In fact the apprenticeship system was ended in 1838. From that date all the former slaves were free to get jobs wherever they liked. The Act was passed just in time to comfort the dying moments of William Wilberforce, who had spent much of his long life campaigning on behalf of slaves. On the other hand, some people resented the fact that the government had handed over £20 million to rich slave-owners, instead of using it to improve the life of poor people in Britain.

The Factory Act of 1833

Parliament also tried to help Britain's factory children. Constant complaints were made to Parliament that in spite of the law (see Chapter 3) factory owners were still making children work long hours. In 1832 Michael Sadler, MP for Aldborough, introduced a new Bill. He proposed that the permitted hours of work for children and young people should be reduced from twelve a day to ten. Many members were uneasy. They knew that Sadler hoped to get a ten-hour day for adults. They were against this, but did not want to vote against a Bill which reduced the hours worked by children. They

therefore appointed a Select Committee and a Royal Commission, both of which interviewed many factory workers.

The 1833 Reports

The reports that the investigators made showed that conditions were worse than many MPs had realised. They found that in some mills children were continually ill-treated. One cloth worker said he had seen 'the girls strapped, but the boys were beat so that they fell to the floor in the course of the beating, with a rope with four tails called a cat'. Usually children were punished because they arrived late in the morning or made mistakes in their work. They were often too tired to do anything else. Eliza Marshall, who had begun work in a Leeds flax mill as a piecer (see page 30) at the age of eight, for four shillings a week, worked from six in the morning until seven at night. She was so tired at night that she had to be carried home, and was 'worse in the morning', when she was woken at half past five by the factory bell ringing. She had, she said 'cried many an hour at the factory'.

By the time she was seventeen Eliza was a cripple, with an iron on her right leg. Parliament was told that this happened to many piecers, because in order to see what they were doing, they had to stoop down, bending the right knee inwards. As they grew up their knees became more and more crooked, until in the end they could hardly walk. It was 'great misery' for Eliza to do her work. Even if children were not actually crippled, their health was often damaged by factory work. An Aberdeen clergyman noticed that working long hours in a stuffy factory made them 'pale and sallow, and generally altered the tone of their voice, which became hoarse'. To make matters worse, many lived in wretched houses and did not get enough to eat. An Aberdeen doctor thought that a large number only had 'a few very indifferent potatoes with a little salt for dinner'. In general the reports painted a miserable picture of the life of factory children. Yet a few children stood up well to the work. Twelve-year-old Catherine Murray worked twelve and a half hours a day in an Aberdeen mill, and then went

Children queue up for their money at the end of the week. Sometimes, when their parents were out of work, children's pay had to keep the whole family

to night school for a hour. She had no complaints, and was 'never very tired at night'. But she was an exception. The committee's report convinced MPs that something would have to be done. What was more, to the delight of most MPs, the commission also recommended a scheme by which hours of work for young children could be cut without affecting those worked by adults.

Clauses of the Act

Their proposals were these. First, no children under the age of nine should be employed in any textile factory using power-driven machinery. Second, those between nine and thirteen should not be allowed to work more than nine hours in any day or forty-eight hours a week, while those between thirteen and eighteen should have their hours limited to twelve a day. Third, all children under the age of thirteen should have to attend school for two hours a day. Fourth, inspectors should be appointed to make sure that the law was enforced. The commissioners took it for granted that most factory owners would keep their mills open for twelve hours a day and employ two shifts of children aged between nine and thirteen for six hours each. By the time the commissioners reported to the Commons, Sadler had lost his seat, and his place as leader of the Ten Hours movement in the Commons had been taken by Lord Ashley. He did not think the commissioners went far enough, but most MPs were pleased with the report and quickly passed a new Factory Act along the lines laid down. It became law in the summer of 1833.

The effects of the Act

The new Act was very unpopular. It disappointed those who wanted a ten-hour day. On the other hand many parents were annoyed that their youngest children were prevented from adding to the family's income by going out to work. Owners of cotton and wool mills felt that they had been treated unfairly. They complained that hours of work in other factories

55

were as long, or even longer. One MP pointed out that

> children employed in the earthernware and porcelain manufactures worked from twelve to fifteen hours per day; file cutters, nail-makers, forgers and colliers worked for twelve hours a day; those engaged in calico printing worked for twelve, fourteen, fifteen and sixteen hours per day; needlemakers, manufacturers of arms and pin-makers worked for thirteen and fourteen hours per day.

Yet none of these were controlled by the 1833 Act.

The new law did not work well. Most mill owners did not bother to employ younger children in shifts. Instead, they dismissed those who were obviously under thirteen, and kept the rest working for twelve hours a day. Many under-age children were kept at work because there was no certain way to prove the age of a child. Children between nine and thirteen had to provide a doctor's certificate. This was no use because a number of people without any medical qualifications set up as doctors just to sell certificates to anyone who asked for them. Workers between thirteen and eighteen were expected to provide certificates of baptism, and one inspector wrote of being offered 'scraps of paper, dirtied and in tatters' which were supposed to come from ministers or priests 'in distant parts of the United Kingdom as justification for the employment of children for twelve hours who were manifestly much under thirteen years of age'. The inspector reckoned that about half the children who claimed to be thirteen were, in fact, twelve or under.

The inspectors also found it difficult to make sure that all children under thirteen went to school for two hours a day. Some mill owners built fine schools and employed good teachers. Others set up a school in an odd corner of the works and put one of their workmen in charge

Some working children in towns were taught reading, writing, arithmetic and religion in 'ragged schools', which were set up and controlled by the Ragged School Union. Lord Ashley was an active member

of it. In one mill an inspector found that the school was in the coal-cellar, with the stoker acting as teacher. In many places 'schools' were set up outside the works. In such places the 'teachers' did nothing more than provide the certificates of attendance. An inspector saw one which ran, 'This is to sertify that 1838 thomas Cordingley as atend martha insep school tow hours per day January 6.'

The inspectors also had problems because there were so few of them. When they arrived in an area, mill owners passed the word round, so that there was plenty of time to send under-age children home before the inspector arrived. But even if they were caught red-handed, mill owners often found that magistrates were on their side, and they often got away with being fined as little as £1. Gradually, however, things improved. More inspectors were appointed, new regulations were made, and the law was better enforced. For instance, in 1836 Parliament passed an Act which eventually made it much easier for the inspectors to fix the age of factory workers. This Act laid down that all births, marriages and deaths had to be registered. Everyone born in Britain was now given an official certificate recording his or her exact date of birth.

The Poor Law Amendment Act, 1834

The old Poor Law

In England in the eighteenth century members of the gentry who had been appointed by the government to act as Justices of the Peace had the job of seeing that the poor were properly cared for. To pay for this, all householders had to pay a tax called the poor rate. Poor people who received money from the rates were known as paupers. Only people who had been 'settled' in a parish for at least forty days had the right to obtain help, and the JPs could make newcomers who had no jobs and seemed unable to support themselves leave the parish. This settlement rule was bad, because it discouraged unemployed labourers from travelling about to look for work. It was safest to stay in your own parish.

In most parishes the JPs set up a poor house—a kind of hostel for poor people who were too old or too ill to look after themselves. But the justices also had the power to pay money out of the rates to poor people who were still living in their own homes. This was known as 'outdoor relief'.

The Speenhamland System

It had been taken for granted that only the unemployed could get help from the rates, but in 1795 the harvest was bad, and the price of bread rose. The JPs in Speenhamland in Berkshire noticed that the wages of many farm labourers were so low that the men could not afford to buy enough bread to feed their families. The JPs decided that even though the labourers were working, they were entitled to receive money from the rates. They laid down that every man must have enough to buy three gallons of bread a week for himself and one and a half for each member of his family. If his pay was too low to buy this quantity, they made it up to the required amount out of the rates. Magistrates in other parishes followed the example of the Berkshire JPs, and the Speenhamland System, as it was called, spread widely over southern England.

The results of the Speenhamland System were bad. It was very expensive. The total poor rate levied rose from less than £2 million a year in 1780 to more than £6 million in 1815. The system encouraged farmers to pay very low wages because they knew that, however little they paid them, their labourers would be given enough money from the rates to live on. It annoyed the other ratepayers, who thought it wrong that they should pay high rates just because farmers would not pay their labourers a living wage. The system also had a very bad effect on the labourers. They were now all paupers, depending for their living on money from the poor rates. This was a terrible blow to their self-respect. To make matters worse, the amount they were paid each week depended entirely on the size of their families. It made no difference how hard they worked. A single man got very little. A man with a large family got much more, however little work he did.

The only thing to be said in favour of the system was that it made sure that labourers and their families had enough to eat. But even this was not always true. As the years passed the magistrates tried to save money by reducing the amount of bread they thought a labouring family needed. By 1820 it was in many places only half what the Speenhamland magistrates had suggested in 1795.

The new Poor Law

Most people agreed that the Speenhamland System was unsatisfactory. In 1832 the government appointed a commission to investigate how the Poor Law worked. In 1834 they reported, recommending that it should be reformed. Parliament agreed, and passed the Poor Law Amendment Act, which completely changed the system. 'Outdoor relief' was abolished for those fit enough to work. In future if they wanted help from the Poor Law they had to enter a workhouse. To cut down on the number applying for relief, conditions in workhouses were to be made worse than those of the lowest paid workers outside. In the words of one official, their policy was to make the workhouses 'a terror to the poor and prevent them entering'. A board of three commissioners was appointed to enforce the new law from their headquarters in London. This board appointed various regional commissioners. At parish level control of the Poor Law was taken out of the hands of the JPs. Instead, parishes were grouped together in 'unions'. Each union had its own workhouse administered by a board of guardians elected by the local ratepayers.

Within a few months the first workhouses were being built in the south of England. It was not until 1837 that the system was introduced

A refuge where the homeless poor could spend the night sleeping under shelter on dry straw instead of in the streets

58

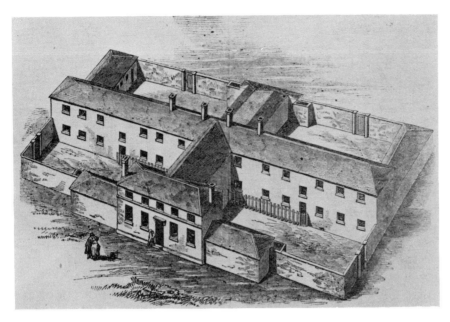

A bird's-eye view of Andover Workhouse. One side was for men, the other for women. Many workhouse buildings still survive. Some are used as hospitals

in the north of the country. Each town had its own workhouse, usually on the outskirts where land was cheap. Villages had to share, and as a result country workhouses were often situated at a crossroads within easy reach of all the villages in the union.

The buildings, surrounded by a high brick wall, were large and plain, like a prison or barracks. Inside, the rooms were bare and cold with white-washed walls. There was no comfortable furniture. In the dining-room there were long wooden tables with benches on either side. The dormitories had rough wooden bedsteads and straw mattresses. The day-rooms, where paupers who were not fit enough to work spent their time, were furnished with hard wooden chairs and benches.

When a family went into a workhouse it was immediately split up. The women and young children were kept quite separate from the men. All their possessions were taken from them and they were given thick, plain workhouse clothes to wear. If they were fit they were put to work like convicts in a prison. Stone-breaking, corn-grinding, bone-crushing and unpicking old rope were all common jobs for workhouse inmates. They were given regular meals of soup, potatoes, bread and occasionally a little cheese or meat. Meals had to be eaten in

silence. Paupers were not allowed out of the workhouse, which made it difficult for them to find a job. They could only receive visitors in the presence of the workhouse master or matron. All alcoholic drinks were banned in workhouses, and paupers were forbidden to smoke. When a pauper died, he was buried as cheaply as possible, in a flimsy coffin crammed into a narrow, shallow grave.

The commissioners, and especially their secretary, Edwin Chadwick, constantly checked local boards to make sure that workhouse conditions were worse than those of the lowest paid labourers, and to prevent 'outdoor relief' being paid to the able-bodied. They were determined to make sure that all over the country the poor were treated alike. In spite of their efforts the treatment of the poor still varied from place to place. In some workhouses paupers were ill-treated and half starved. One or two masters were brutal and beat them, while at Andover Workhouse in Hampshire inmates were so badly fed that they fought over scraps of gristle sticking to the bones they were crushing. In other unions the guardians tried to treat the poor humanely and to make sure that they were properly fed. The commissioners were also unable to do away with 'outdoor relief'. In northern industrial towns a sudden slump in trade could throw large numbers of men out of work all at once—far too many to bring into the workhouse. These men still had to be helped by cash payments. Even in the rural south it was often easier and cheaper to pay labourers in cash for a few weeks than to force them into the workhouse. Many boards of guardians did this, in spite of the commissioners.

Financially the new law was a success. In 1831 nearly £7 million had been spent on the poor rates. In 1851 this sum had fallen to below £5 million, in spite of a rise of 29 per cent in the population. The number of paupers had also fallen. This was partly because the 1834 Act had altered the settlement rule. It was now easier for men to leave their own parishes to look for work. What was more, there was a good deal of work available. For instance, the railway builders had taken on a large number of navvies. So it was not only fear of the workhouse that reduced the number of paupers. None the less, the workers hated the new system. In some ways paupers were now treated worse than criminals, and the workhouses were often nick-named 'Bastilles' after the French prison that was burnt down in the Revolution in 1789. Gradually, however, the system was reformed. In 1842 husbands and wives were allowed to stay together in the workhouse. Talking was permitted at mealtimes. Schools were provided for the children and in 1847 the three commissioners were replaced by a Poor Law Board who continued to improve conditions, particularly for the children and the elderly.

The Municipal Corporations Act, 1835

Once the Reform Act had been passed, the government decided to investigate the borough corporations. There were more than 200 boroughs in England and Wales. These had been granted royal charters which gave each of them the right to send MPs to Parliament and to elect a corporation. This corporation was expected to supervise trade, control borough finances and provide magistrates to keep law and order. By 1833 these corporations varied a good deal. In some places they were elected by all ratepayers. In others, only members of the corporation itself had the right to vote in corporation elections. In a few places—King's Lynn was one example—corporations were very efficient, but in many they were corrupt and did as little work as possible. Some met only to elect the MP for the borough. Others spent a good deal of time discussing what they should do with the land and money which was owned by the borough. They often used much of it to pay for feasts and celebrations for themselves.

There was no doubt that the system needed reform, and in 1833 the government appointed a number of lawyers to inquire into English and Welsh boroughs. The lawyers reported in 1835. They found that most corporations were inefficient, corrupt and out of touch with the people living in the towns. So the government passed the Municipal Corporations Act. In future, towns were to be governed by councillors, who were to be elected by all the ratepayers, and by a small number of aldermen, to be appointed by the council. All the funds of the borough were to be under the control of the council, which was also to be responsible for providing a police force. Any large town which wished to become a borough could apply for a charter. In Scotland, where the Burgh Reform Act had been passed in 1833, the right to elect councillors was given to £10 householders—the same as for parliamentary elections.

The Municipal Reform Act had important results. So far as party politics were concerned, the Whigs gained, because many of the old corporations had been controlled by the Tories. In the towns themselves, the new councils paid a good deal of attention to the wishes of the ratepayers they represented. This was not always a good thing. Some councils thought that their main duty was to keep the rates down and therefore did nothing to improve the town they were governing. But as time went on the new councils gradually took on more and more jobs. There was certainly plenty for them to do. For instance, most industrial towns had little drinking water, no sewers, no street lights, no town halls and no libraries. The new corporations eventually provided all of these.

STOCKTON UNION.

Dietary for able-bodied Men and Women.

		BREAKFAST.		DINNER.				SUPPER.	
		Bread.	Boiled Milk with Oatmeal.	Cooked Meat.	Potatoes.	Suet Pudding.	Soup or Rice Milk.	Bread.	Boiled Milk with Oatmeal or Broth.
		Ozs.	Pints.	Ozs.	lbs.	Ozs.	Pints.	Ozs.	Pints.
Sunday	Men	6	1½	....	....	14	....	6	1½
	Women	6	1½	....	....	14	....	6	1½
Monday	Men	6	1½	5	¾	....	....	6	1½
	Women	6	1½	5	¾	....		6	1½
Tuesday	Men	6	1½	....	....	....	1½	6	1½
	Women	6	1½	....	....	....	1½	6	1½
Wednesday	Men	6	1½	....	....	14	....	6	1½
	Women	6	1½	....	....	14	....	6	1½
Thursday	Men	6	1½	....	....	....	1½	6	1½
	Women	6	1½	....	....	....	1½	6	1½
Friday	Men	6	1½	5	¾	....	....	6	1½
	Women	6	1½	5	¾	....	....	6	1½
Saturday	Men	6	1½	....	....	....	1½	6	1½
	Women	6	1½	....	....	....	1½	6	1½

Old People above 60 years of age, may be allowed Tea, Coffee, Butter, and Sugar, (not exceeding 1 oz. of Tea, 2 oz. of Coffee, 3½ oz. of Butter, and 4 oz. of Sugar, per week each) in lieu of Gruel to Breakfast. Greens, occasionally, in lieu of Potatoes.

4 oz. of Bread to Soup and Rice Milk Dinners, to each Person.

Children under 9 years of age dieted at discretion. Sick dieted as ordered by the Medical Officer.

A workhouse diet sheet in the middle of the nineteenth century. Meat was only served twice a week

7 Chartism

Working-class discontent

For the first few years after the Reform Act of 1832 harvests were good, food was cheap and trade was booming. Most workers were reasonably prosperous and contented. In 1836, however, all this changed. There was a slump in trade and a poor harvest. Food prices rose. Some men lost their jobs: others had their pay reduced. They all found that it was costing more to feed themselves and their families. Times were bad, and as usual, ordinary working people suffered more than the rest. Many of them felt angry and thought that Parliament had let them down. The Reform Act, which they had supported, had not given them the vote. Workers had set up committees and petitioned Parliament to limit their hours of work to ten a day. But the Factory Act of 1833 still allowed them to work twelve. Parliament had given money to West Indian slave-owners, which could have been used to improve British towns. Finally, the new Poor Law passed in 1834 meant that if any workers lost their jobs, they might well have to go into one of the hated new workhouses. To make matters worse, Robert Owen's Grand National Consolidated Trades Union, which might have been able to help them, had collapsed.

Some working men believed that the only answer to their problems was to give ordinary workers the vote and the right to sit in Parliament. In 1836 a number of them set up the London Working Men's Association. Its most important member, William Lovett, a cabinet-maker, was a thoughtful man who believed that in the end they would get what they wanted by peaceful persuasion. Most of the members of his association were also steady, sensible men. They got in touch with members of the Birmingham Political Union, which, under the lead of Thomas Attwood, MP, had been fighting for the reform of Parliament since 1830, and together they drew up the People's Charter, which was published in 1838.

The People's Charter

The Charter had six points, all of which were designed to help workers to get into Parliament. First, it laid down that all men over the age of twenty-one should have the vote. Second, the vote was to be by secret ballot. Workers would not then be frightened to vote against the wishes of their masters. Third, the property qualification for MPs was to be abolished, so that workers who owned no property could enter Parliament. Fourth, it demanded payment for members. Workers and tradesmen would then be able to give up their jobs to become MPs and still make a living. Fifth, all constituencies were to be the same size. This would mean that the big industrial towns, where there were a lot of workers, would get more seats. Sixth, a fresh Parliament was to be elected every year to make sure that MPs did what the electors wanted.

Lovett and O'Connor

In August 1838 a meeting was held in Birmingham to launch the Charter. It did not go quite as Lovett and his friends had hoped. They wanted to win over the 'most intelligent and influential portion' of the working classes by reasoned argument. They found that they were opposed by a large number of delegates from the north-east of England and the East Mid-

The Six Points
OF THE
PEOPLE'S
CHARTER.

1. A VOTE for every man twenty-one years of age, of sound mind, and not undergoing punishment for crime.

2. THE BALLOT.—To protect the elector in the exercise of his vote.

3. No PROPERTY QUALIFICATION for Members of Parliament —thus enabling the constituencies to return the man of their choice, be he rich or poor.

4. PAYMENT OF MEMBERS, thus enabling an honest trades- man, working man, or other person, to serve a constituency, when taken from his business to attend to the interests of the country.

5. EQUAL CONSTITUENCIES, securing the same amount of representation for the same number of electors, instead of allowing small constituencies to swamp the votes of large ones.

6. ANNUAL PARLIAMENTS, thus presenting the most effectual check to bribery and intimidation, since though a constituency might be bought once in seven years (even with the ballot), no purse could buy a constituency (under a system of universal suffrage) in each ensuing twelvemonth; and since members, when elected for a year only, would not be able to defy and betray their constituents as now.

Subjoined are the names of the gentlemen who embodied these principles into the document called the "People's Charter," at an influential meeting held at the British Coffee House, London, on the 7th of June, 1837:—

Daniel O'Connell, Esq., M.P.,	Mr. Henry Hetherington.
John Arthur Roebuck, Esq., M.P.	Mr. John Cleave.
John Temple Leader, Esq., M.P.	Mr. James Watson.
Charles Hindley, Esq., M.P.	Mr. Richard Moore.
Thomas Perronet Thompson, Esq., M.P.	Mr. William Lovett.
William Sharman Crawford, Esq., M.P.	Mr. Henry Vincent.

W. COLLINS, PRINTER, "WEEKLY TIMES" OFFICE, DUDLEY.

This leaflet, distributed in 1837, sets out the six points of the Charter and gives the names of those who drew it up

An artist's impression of Feargus O'Connor making a speech

lands. Many of these men belonged to trades like hand-loom weaving or wool-combing which were hit hard by the growth of factories, and they had no time for reason and persuasion. They wanted the points of the Charter to be granted without delay and, if all else failed, they were prepared to begin an armed rebellion to get what they wanted. Lovett would have nothing to do with physical force. He believed in what he called 'moral force'.

The leader of the 'physical force' Chartists was an Irish politician named Feargus O'Connor, a giant of a man. He had a voice like a trumpet and a quick wit. He loved long words. Once, in the middle of a speech, he turned on a small group who were hissing him and said, 'You, gentlemen, belong to the big-bellied, little-brained, numbskull aristocracy. How dare you hiss me, you contemptible set of platter-faced, amphibious politicians?' He spoke with great sympathy of the sufferings of the poor. He was, he said, the champion of 'the fustian jackets, blistered hands and unshorn chins'. His speeches were very popular. He also ran a weekly paper called the *Northern Star*, which became the official Chartist newspaper. By the end of 1838 it had a circulation of 50,000 copies.

The first petition

In 1838 O'Connor and his supporters were in a majority. They decided to go back to their own parts of the country, call meetings to elect members for a National Convention in London in the new year, and prepare a huge petition to Parliament in favour of the Charter. In February 1839 the convention met. Unfortunately, once they had come together, they were unable to decide what they ought to do if Parliament rejected their petition, which had well over a million signatures. Some wanted the convention to become a kind of rival Parliament. Others called for a general strike, while a few were in favour of armed rebellion—'universal suffrage or death'. Some of the speeches frightened delegates who believed only in 'moral force', and they went home.

For various reasons the House of Commons did not consider the Chartist petition until July 1839, when it rejected it by 235 votes to 46. This was not surprising, for both the Whigs and the Tories were against giving workers the vote. By the end of July, the government had been able to take precautions. In the south, Lovett and several other Chartist leaders were arrested and imprisoned. In the north, Sir Charles Napier, who had been put in charge of the troops there, invited Chartist leaders to a demonstration of artillery fire. He pointed out to them that if they did begin a rising, it would easily be crushed. 'Poor people,' he wrote afterwards, 'they will suffer. We have the physical force, not they.' In September the convention was dissolved. There was no general strike, and no large-scale rebellion.

The attack on Newport

There was, however, trouble in South Wales. On 3 November John Frost, a draper who had once been Mayor of Newport, led a band of Welsh miners in an attack on the town. He had been a member of the Chartist Convention and seems to have believed that his rising would be supported by a rebellion in the north of England led by O'Connor. But O'Connor refused to have anything to do with Frost's plans, and went off on a visit to Ireland at the end of October. Frost's attack failed. Twenty-four of his followers were killed and he and two others were arrested, tried and sentenced to death. After numerous meetings and petitions the sentences were changed to transportation for life.

In 1840, trade picked up and the country became more prosperous. There was less discontent, and support for the Charter declined. The leaders realised that to be really effective they needed to be better organised, and they set up the National Charter Association to found local branches and help them to organise their activities. Many branches were badly run, but some succeeded in organising meetings and marches to keep interest in the Charter alive.

Chartist meetings

Some Chartist meetings were huge. On public holidays there were open-air rallies. Men would come from every town in the neighbourhood, marching along the roads to the rallying place. Often they sang as they marched and the *Northern Star* regularly printed Chartist verses to be sung to well-known tunes. The following, which appeared in 1841, was set to the tune of 'Rule Britannia':

> Let Britain's heralds take their stand,
> And loudly through the isle proclaim,
> This is the Charter of the land;
> While million voices shout the same.
> Hail Britannia! Britannia's sons are free!
> Suffrage guards their liberty.

Some groups had their own brass bands, and most had colourful banners. All through the morning the Chartists would assemble. Most brought their families with them. Stalls and booths were set up, until the meeting place looked like a fairground. In the afternoon came the speeches. Usually only a few of those present could hear what was said but they all joined in the cheering and clapping, and at the end of the day went home with their faith in the Charter renewed.

Sometimes Chartists held evening meetings in manufacturing towns. As a rule these meetings were preceded by a torchlight procession through the town. A Chartist wrote many years later that the men made 'the heavens echo with the thunder of their cheers' when they recognised one of their leaders watching them march past, while they gave 'volleys of the most hideous groans on passing the office of some hostile newspaper, or the house of some obnoxious magistrate or employer'. Many banners had skulls and cross-bones painted on them, which showed up well in the flickering torchlight. Some men in the procession would have come straight from their work with no time to wash or change. Their faces 'begrimed with sweat and dirt, added to the strange aspect of the scene'. The lights carried by the marchers lit up the sky, and when they reached the meeting place to hear the speeches, the huge number of blazing torches seemed to 'inflame the minds alike of speaker and hearers'.

Torchlight processions and holiday meetings were difficult to organise and could not be held very often. To keep interest alive, local groups had talks and discussions, which were often based on articles from the *Northern Star*. Sometimes Chartists invaded meetings of other organisations and took them over. In 1841, for instance, a number burst into a missionary society meeting in Norwich. One of them took charge of the meeting, but was arrested and removed by a policeman. Those who had come to the original meeting were now arguing with the Chartists, who started shouting, 'We want more pigs and less parsons!' Neither side would give way, and in the end they all went home. It seemed that nothing had been achieved, but as the affair was reported in the local paper, the Chartists did get some free publicity.

The second petition

In 1842, trade slumped once again. Indeed, according to most historians, conditions were even worse than they had been in 1836. As

There were serious riots in Preston in 1842. A magistrate read the Riot Act, but the rioters refused to disperse, and two of them were shot by soldiers

more workers supported the Chartists, O'Connor decided to draw up another petition to present to Parliament. He toured the country making speeches, claiming that this petition would succeed, and that all the problems of the working classes would somehow be solved. By the beginning of May 1842 the petition, signed by over 3 million people, was ready, and was presented to the House of Commons. It was rejected by 287 votes to 49. Once again MPs showed that they were opposed to giving votes to working men.

O'Connor had no idea what to do next. Many disappointed Chartists went on strike, and there were riots, especially in the north. In Lancashire gangs of workers went round factories and knocked the drain plugs out of boilers, which brought the factories to a complete standstill. This outbreak was known as the 'Plug Plot'. Troops had to be sent to restore order, and the strikers' leaders were arrested, tried and transported. O'Connor did not approve of these strikes and riots, but could not suggest any other means by which the workers could make their feelings known. He was criticised from all sides. Once again, as in 1839, he had roused the Chartists to action, and had

achieved nothing. He was very upset. He wrote in the *Northern Star* about those leaders who described Chartists as 'the dupes of Feargus O'Connor', and described himself as 'loved and respected, aye, even adored by the working classes in consequence of his devotion to them and their cause'. But however devoted he was, nothing could hide the fact that he had failed.

The Chartist land scheme

From 1842 onwards, trade slowly revived. As a result, the demand for reform steadily declined once more. O'Connor found that the Charter was less popular. He therefore began to put forward a new, quite different scheme to make working people independent. He set up a fund to which workers subscribed money. This fund was used to buy land, which was let in four-acre lots (1½ hectares) to some of the subscribers. The rent they paid also went into the fund. O'Connor believed that in the end there would be enough money to provide every subscriber with a plot of land. The scheme was very popular. Many a worker thought that if only he had a bit of land to farm, he would be his own master instead of a slave to what a Chartist poet called 'The Steam King'. O'Connor became very popular and in 1847 was elected to Parliament as MP for Nottingham. Meanwhile the money flowed in, and the Chartist Co-operative Land Society, founded in 1845, bought an estate near Watford in Hertfordshire in 1846. The other Chartist leaders disliked the scheme. They saw that it would be difficult to administer, and believed that it had nothing to do with the aims of the Charter. They proved to be right. In order to buy the Watford estate, the society had been forced to borrow money, and if the fund was to pay off its debts it needed every penny it could get. Unfortunately many of the subscribers found that their small-holdings did not pay and they could not afford the rent. To make matters worse, O'Connor did not bother to keep proper accounts and in 1848 the whole scheme was found to be bankrupt.

The third petition

At the beginning of 1848 the hopes of the Chartists were high. Trade was slack and discontent was widespread. In February there was a revolution in France, in which the king, Louis-Philippe, was overthrown. This encouraged the Chartist leaders and they called a general convention to draw up another petition to Parliament. The convention met on 3 April. Some members seemed to be in favour of armed rebellion, but O'Connor was not. In the end they decided to organise a great demonstration on 10 April. There was to be a mass meeting on Kennington Common in south London, with speeches, and then a huge procession to escort the petition across the Thames to the House of Commons. The authorities were very alarmed at this news. They knew that some Chartist leaders had advised their followers to carry arms, and they were afraid that there might be a pitched battle in the streets of London. The government asked the Duke of Wellington, who was nearly eighty, to take charge of the defence of the city, and banned the procession.

In spite of the ban, the Chartists decided to go ahead with their plans. But nothing seemed to go right. Chartism was not particularly popular in London, so the crowd was much smaller than expected. Only 23,000 people

A group of Chartists escort the main speakers to the meeting at Kennington in 1848

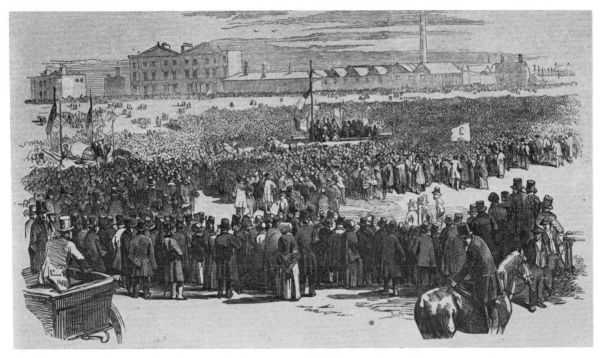

At Kennington the crowd gather round the cart on which the main speakers are standing

assembled on the Common. The Chartists had hoped for 100,000. Moreover, Wellington's plans for defending the capital were very effective. He had some troops hidden away in case they were needed, but to keep order in the streets he had set up a force of 170,000 special constables, most of them middle-class Londoners, wearing white badges and armed with wooden staves. Many of these constables were stationed on the bridges over the Thames which the procession would have to cross on its way to the Commons. O'Connor knew that the Chartist procession would not get through, and in his speech to the meeting, he advised them to go home. He explained that the police had given permission for the petition to be taken to Parliament in a cab, escorted by a small number of leading Chartists. There were some angry protests but these were cut short by heavy rain. The disappointed Chartists streamed away. Those who wished to cross the river found that they were only allowed on the bridges a few at a time. Crowds gathered, pushing and jostling. The police moved in with their staves and cracked a few heads. Gradually the

crowds dispersed, and in a short time London was quiet again.

Meanwhile, the petition, said to contain nearly 6 million signatures, was loaded into its cab, and the delegates who were to accompany it clambered into a large van drawn by six farm horses. They set off, and in due course reached Westminster where the petition, which had been rolled up into four large bundles, was unloaded and carried into the House of Commons. It was an undignified end to a disappointing day.

There was worse to come. Instead of rejecting the Chartist petition, the House of Commons appointed a special committee to examine it. They found that instead of nearly 6 million signatures it contained only about 2 million. Many seemed to be in the same handwriting and included the names of the Queen, the Duke of Wellington and Mr Punch. Some names were clearly made up, like 'No-cheese', 'Pug-nose' or 'Flat-nose'. There were others which were so obscene that the committee would not 'hazard offending the House' by repeating them. It was difficult to take Chartism

68

seriously any longer. The great demonstration had failed, the petition was a fraud, and the land scheme bankrupt. O'Connor was a broken man. In 1852 he had a mental breakdown, and in 1855 he died. Ernest Jones took over, and tried his best to keep the movement alive but in 1860 the National Charter Association was finally closed down.

The failure of Chartism

The Chartists had gained none of the points for which they had fought. They were not to know that five of the six were to be granted later. As far as they were concerned, they had failed. It is easy to see why. In the first place, though the Chartists agreed that the working class ought to have a greater say in how the country was governed, they disagreed on almost everything else. Some thought that once the workers had gained power they ought to use it to destroy the factory system. Others, like Lovett, believed that machines and factories could be used to create wealth to make workers richer and more contented than ever before. The Chartists also quarrelled about tactics. Lovett and his supporters believed in a campaign of quiet persuasion. O'Connor preferred large crowds, long processions and threats of violent revolution. These disagreements had a very bad effect on Chartism. In Scotland, for instance, Glasgow and Edinburgh Chartists argued so violently with one another that they found it almost impossible to work together.

A really skilled leader might have been able to overcome these disagreements. Unfortunately Lovett was unable to inspire a crowd, and though O'Connor was a good orator, he was tactless and conceited. This made the divisions worse. O'Connor was also very unreliable. When speaking or writing he was full of vague threats of violence and revolution. But whenever it seemed that there might be a real confrontation between the Chartists and the government, O'Connor backed down, leaving his supporters high and dry. In spite of his failings he always took it for granted that whatever he did was bound to succeed. This meant that when he failed, he had no idea what to do next.

But, in any case, the Charter did not appeal to the majority of the British people. The upper and middle classes did not like it because they did not want to share their power with the workers. This was shown very clearly in 1848 when the London middle classes enrolled as special constables to oppose the Chartist march. This lack of middle-class support was a grave disadvantage, because the Chartists badly needed the organising skill of tradesmen, merchants and manufacturers. Many workers did not support the Charter. As long as they had secure, well-paid jobs, it did not matter much to them that they did not have a vote. So the Chartists could only be sure of mass support when trade was bad and work was scarce. At other times support tended to fade away.

From 1845 onwards many workers were much better off. There were plenty of jobs available building the railways (see Chapter 9), while a succession of good harvests and the repeal of the Corn Law (see Chapter 8) resulted in lower food prices. Chartism also had to face competition from a number of new trade unions which were working to improve factory conditions, and from Co-operative Societies. The members of these societies clubbed together to open shops, which sold good-quality products at reasonable prices. Any profits were distributed to the customers and to society members. Many working people thought down-to-earth activities like this more sensible than marching through the streets demanding the vote.

The Chartists failed to achieve what they wanted. Yet what they did had important consequences. It was probably their activities that persuaded the government to speed up improvements in living and working conditions for the working classes, in the hope that once they were more comfortable, they would stop asking for the vote. The 1839 demonstrations certainly led to the 1839 Rural Police Act, which established the first professional police forces outside London. Finally, and perhaps most important, other working-class leaders learned from the Chartists. Later leaders understood the importance of unity of purpose and good organisation. Their success was built on the failure of Chartism.

8 Peel and Free Trade

Politics, 1835–1841

Between 1835 and 1841 great changes took place in British politics. In 1837 William IV died, and his niece, Victoria, became queen at the age of eighteen. Though Victoria had her faults, she was a great improvement on her uncles. Above all, she was respectable, and for the first time for nearly thirty years Britain was ruled by somebody whose private life set a good example to the people. There was also a new

Lord Ashley succeeded his father as Earl of Shaftesbury in 1851. He helped to pass various Factory Acts and the Mines Act. His longest fight was to make it illegal to send children up chimneys to sweep them clean with a hand brush. This was not finally stopped until 1875

Prime Minister. In 1834 Grey was replaced by Lord Melbourne. He believed that the country needed time to settle down after all the changes of recent years. There were therefore very few reforms until 1841 when the Whigs were defeated and the Tories came back to power, with Sir Robert Peel as Prime Minister.

Since 1832 Peel had been working hard to change the Tory party. In 1834, in a manifesto addressed to his constituents in Tamworth, he made it clear that he accepted the Reform Act of 1832, and showed that he was prepared to support other reforms where they were needed. This new Toryism became known as Conservatism, and many look on Peel as one of the founders of the modern Conservative party. Most people respected him. He worked very hard, had a marvellous memory and was very intelligent. But few people liked him. Queen Victoria thought him 'an odd, cold man'. Lord Ashley, too, was struck by his coldness. Peel, he said, was 'an iceberg with a slight thaw on the surface'. Wellington was more brutal. 'The trouble is,' he told a friend, 'that Peel has no manners.'

Peel's free trade budget

When Peel came to power in 1841, he found that the country's finances were in a bad state. Nobody in the Whig governments which had been in office since 1830 really understood finance, and when they found the country short of money they increased taxes on goods to raise the cash they needed. These higher taxes, known as duties, had increased the cost of living and discouraged trade. Peel decided that the best way out of this difficulty was to reduce the rates of duty. To help manufacturers he first

70

At the pit bottom, a miner hooked the baskets of coal onto a rope, and an engine wound them to the surface. The miners travelled up and down in the same baskets

cut duties on the raw materials they imported. These cuts meant that to begin with, less money was coming in to the government. To make up for this, Peel brought in income tax, for three years only, at seven pence in the pound. His policy worked, and in 1845 he abolished or reduced many other duties. Peel's measures were a great success. They helped industry, increased trade and reduced the cost of living.

The Mines Report of 1842

Peel's government also tried to improve working conditions. First, they turned their attention to the coal-mines. The demand for coal had been growing since 1750. As the population grew, more coal was used for domestic heating, and huge quantities were needed to smelt iron, and fuel the new steam-engines. So existing mines were deepened and extended, and many new ones were opened to try to keep pace with the demand.

Working conditions were very bad. Mines were dark, dusty, cramped, hot and dangerous. Visitors who went down a pit thought it a great adventure as they were lowered down the shaft in pitch darkness in a basket. Once they were at the bottom, they had to find their way 'through passage after passage in the blackest darkness' which was made 'more awful by a death-like silence, broken by the banging of some distant door'. Strangers were shocked by those they found working in mines, 'most half-naked, blackened all over with dirt, ragged and beastly in their appearance, and with a shameless indecency in their behaviour'.

In most pits in Britain there were men,

women and children at work. The men were hewers, who actually hacked the coal out. Sometimes they used a pickaxe and shovel. Sometimes they hammered wedges into the coal to loosen it. In some pits they drilled holes into the coal and blew it out with gunpowder. There was always a risk that the roof might cave in on them, or that water might suddenly come flooding in. In some pits there were quantities of methane gas which a spark or a candle flame might cause to explode at any time. Even the coal-dust itself sometimes blew up. Where the coal seams were narrow the miners had to crouch or lie down all day. In deep pits it was very warm, and the miners worked naked.

Once miners had loosened the coal, it had to be taken back to the shaft. In some pits this was done by ponies which pulled trucks along a kind of underground railway. In others women and girls were harnessed to the trucks and hauled them by crawling on all fours along low, narrow passages. Patience Kershaw of Halifax, who was seventeen in 1842, worked twelve hours a day moving tubs, each holding 3 hundredweight of coal, about the pit. She pulled some with a belt and chain. She pushed others with her head. This had given her a bald patch. At work she wore trousers and 'a ragged jacket'. The hewers where she worked were naked. The man who interviewed her described her as 'an ignorant, filthy, ragged and deplorable looking object'. She was the only girl in the pit. She would, she said, 'rather work in a mill'. In some Scottish pits the work was even harder, because the girls had to carry coal on their backs up ladders to the surface.

The youngest children in the mine were 'trappers'. They looked after underground doors which divided one part of the pit from another. As a bearer approached with her load, the trapper opened the door. Once she had gone through, he closed it again and waited in the dark until the next one came along. Some of the trappers were as young as five or six. Many, like Sarah Gooder, were only eight. She said she was not tired by her work, but was scared to sit alone in the dark. Another girl who fell asleep for a while said that when she woke the rats had run away with her bread and cheese.

Miners' houses

Coal-miners were usually well paid for their work. They could earn between twenty-five and thirty shillings a week, which was double the wage of farm labourers. In many mining families the wife and children worked as well, so that there was a lot of money coming in. Yet their houses were often wretched. A miner's son, James Taylor, aged eleven, described his house in Oldham in 1842:

> There are two rooms i'th'house—the chamber and th'house. The chamber is above th'house. They all sleep in the chamber, which has one bed, in which all four children sleep with their father and mother. There is one chair in the room besides, but nothing else.

In a miner's house in East Lothian a visitor noticed that nine people slept in two beds: 'The whole of the other furniture consisted of two chairs, three stools, a table, a kail-pot and a few broken basins and cups.'

Miners usually had enough to eat. Patience Kershaw had porridge and milk for breakfast, a cake which she ate at work for her dinner, and then potatoes and meat when she got home, but 'not every day meat'. Many miners were great drunkards. When they had money in their pockets they took a few days off work to go drinking. When they had spent all their cash they went back to work. So they never had any money to save or spend on their homes.

Conditions were not the same all over the country. They were probably best in Northumberland and Durham, where no women or girls had been employed in the pits since 1780, and worst in old pits in the east of Scotland. In 1840 Lord Ashley persuaded Parliament to appoint a commission which inquired into conditions in the mines. In 1842 they published their report. People were shocked to hear about the young trappers, and the heavy work done by girls, and above all, about young girls working alongside naked men.

The Mines Act of 1842

Parliament acted quickly and passed the Mines Act which banned all women and girls from

The 1842 Mines Report was illustrated with woodcuts, which increased its impact. Many people were shocked by this picture of a naked hewer at work

working down mines, and fixed the lower age limit for boys at ten. Inspectors were appointed to see that the Act was enforced. In some places the new law caused hardship. Women who had worked in mines all their lives were suddenly dismissed and could not easily find new jobs. In some cases mine owners gave them their old jobs back. They reckoned it was easy to hide away a few women in a pit when an inspector called. It was therefore several years before there were no females at all working underground.

The Factory Act of 1844

Encouraged by Lord Ashley, Peel's government also passed an important Factory Act in 1844: dangerous machinery now had to be guarded, and the hours of work for children under thirteen were reduced to six and a half a day. But to make up for this, the age at which children could begin work was reduced from nine to eight. Three years later, in 1847, Lord Ashley at last persuaded Parliament to pass an Act limiting the hours of work for women and young people under eighteen to ten a day. All the supporters of the ten hours movement were delighted because they believed that once the women and girls were sent home, men would have to stop work as well. But by using a shift system, the owners found a way round the Act. In the end, in 1851, an agreement was reached by which the hours of work for all those employed in textile mills were limited to ten and a half a day. All these Acts applied only to factories which made cloth, but gradually Parliament began to control conditions in other industries. For example, in 1845 calico-printing mills were brought under the Factory Acts.

The repeal of the Corn Law

Peel's ministry was eventually brought to an end by the Corn Law, which made imported wheat more expensive. This law was becoming more and more unpopular. Some people were against it because they believed that all taxes on food were morally wrong. Many people thought it was unfair that farmers should be protected by a high rate of duty on corn at a time when duties on manufactured goods were being reduced, and argued that the Corn Law showed that landowners had far too much power compared with the rest of society. There were also some manufacturers who believed that if the Corn Law was repealed, the price of bread would fall and they would be able to reduce the amount they paid their workers, thus making higher profits.

The Anti-Corn Law League

In 1839 a few opponents of the Corn Law set up the Anti-Corn Law League, with headquarters in Manchester. Its most important member was Richard Cobden, the son of a Sussex farmer. He had worked as a clerk and as a commercial traveller, and had eventually set up a cloth-printing works in Manchester. He was a good organiser and a clear speaker, and in 1841 he was elected MP for Stockport. Cobden organised the league, and in 1843 he was joined in the Commons by John Bright, who had inherited a Rochdale cloth factory from his father. They worked well together. While Cobden relied on facts and figures to influence the minds of his audience, Bright quoted from poetry and the Bible to work on their feelings.

Most of the members of the league were middle class. Many were manufacturers who believed that the law was bad for trade. Though most working people were also against the Corn Law, they felt it was more important for them to get the vote than to work for the repeal of the Corn Law. They therefore supported the Chartists (see Chapter 7) and were suspicious of the middle-class league, which was richer and much better organised than the Chartists.

The league got its message across in various ways. It published its own weekly paper, and produced pamphlets which were delivered to every elector in Britain, either by hand or by the new penny post (see Chapter 9). Cobden reckoned that over 5 million had been distributed in 1843 alone. The league also held meet-

Daniel O'Connell, the Irish MP, addressing a meeting of the Anti-Corn Law League

ings, and Cobden in particular used to go on long tours, travelling sometimes by rail, but more often by coach. In January 1844 he wrote to his brother from Dundee that he was

nearly overdone with work, two meetings at Aberdeen on Monday, up at four on Tuesday, travelled thirty-five miles, held a meeting at Montrose, and then thirty-five miles more to Dundee for a meeting the same evening. Tomorrow we go to Cupar Fife, next day, Leith, the day following Jedburgh.

Cobden complained that he 'lived in public meetings' and he permanently damaged his voice, so that later in life it was sometimes little more than a hoarse whisper.

Cobden enjoyed his meetings. In most towns the league's supporters flocked to the hall, where tea was served before the meeting began. Then came the speeches, which were followed by a collection. Occasionally in English towns well over £1,000 might be contributed by the audience. In Scotland it was different. 'We found,' Cobden told his wife, 'that to name money was like reading the Riot Act for dispersing them.' This did not much matter, because the league could be sure of a regular supply of money from rich manufacturers. Some meetings were hostile. In country districts Cobden addressed farmers and landowners who supported the Corn Law. At Bedford he spoke to a gathering of 'brutish squires and bullfrogs', while in Sussex he described his audience to his brother as 'chawbacons'. On such occasions he used to ask those present, 'How, when or where have farmers and farm labourers benefited by the Corn Law?' Often nobody could answer him, and sometimes the meeting ended by voting in favour of repeal.

The league certainly affected public opinion. It made people think hard about the Corn Law and persuaded many that it ought to be repealed. But it probably had little or no effect on the policy of the government.

Peel and the Corn Law

The majority of the Conservative party supported the Corn Law. Some of them believed that British farmers would be unable to make a living if foreign corn was allowed in duty free. Others thought that if the Corn Law was repealed, it would show that the government no longer cared so much about the interests of landowners. Peel was not so sure. He thought that if free trade in other goods helped to make the country more prosperous, the same would apply to corn. He knew, however, that any suggestion that the Corn Law should be repealed would break up his party. He was not prepared to take this risk, and at the election in 1841 he had promised that the Corn Law would stay.

As the years passed, Peel's attitude changed. In 1842, he altered the sliding scale so that less duty was paid on foreign corn; by 1845 the success of his free-trade measures and the arguments of the league had convinced him that the Corn Law ought to go. In March he was sitting in the Commons as Cobden was speaking in favour of repeal. Everybody expected Peel to answer Cobden's arguments, but he suddenly crumpled up the notes he was making and turned to Sidney Herbert who was sitting next to him. '*You* must answer this, for *I* cannot,' he said. But though he was now in favour of repealing the Corn Law, Peel was in no hurry. He had no intention of breaking the promise he had made in 1841. Events in Ireland changed his mind.

The potato famine and repeal

All through the early years of the nineteenth century the Irish population continued to grow. By 1841 it had reached over 8 million. Most of these people were peasants who lived on the potatoes they grew on their small plots of land. Usually potatoes did well in Ireland, but in 1845 they were affected by a fungus known as blight, and more than half the crop was destroyed. This was a catastrophe. Without their potatoes, many thousands would starve. Peel acted quickly. At the beginning of November he ordered £100,000 to be spent on buying maize from America. He also decided that, to save the Irish, all kinds of food, including corn, would have to be imported duty free. He demanded 'the total and absolute repeal for

75

ever' of all duties on foodstuffs, including corn. In spite of long discussions, Peel was unable to persuade all his ministers to agree with him. He resigned, and Lord John Russell, the Whig leader, tried to form a government. He failed. Peel was brought back and early in 1846 the Corn Law was repealed. Many Conservatives voted against their leader, while most of the Whigs supported him. But a few days later Peel was beaten on a routine vote in the House of Commons. Seventy of his own party, led by young Mr Disraeli, voted against him. Eighty did not vote at all. The Conservative party was split, and could no longer govern the country. Peel resigned and the Whigs took over. Wellington, for one, was very bitter. 'Rotten potatoes have done it all,' he said.

Effects of repeal

Apart from bringing down the government, the repeal of the Corn Law seemed to have little effect. The farmers did not suffer and the Irish were not helped. The corn harvests of 1845 and 1846 were poor, so that there was none to spare to sell cheaply to the Irish. The maize which Peel bought in 1845 lasted a few months and in the summer of 1846 it seemed that there would be a good potato crop. At the end of July a coastguard on a journey noticed that the potato fields were in full bloom. A week later he passed the same way and found all the leaves in every field 'scorched black'. The blight had struck again. This time it was worse: almost the whole crop was destroyed. The results were horrific.

During the famine many landowners in Ireland evicted tenants who were unable to pay their rent

In December 1846, a magistrate visited the town of Skibbereen and found in one hut

> six famished and ghastly skeletons, huddled in a corner on some filthy straw, their sole covering what seemed a horsecloth. I found by a low moaning they were alive—they were in fever, four children, a woman and what had once been a man.

In another house in the same village the police found two frozen corpses, half eaten by rats. Over most of Ireland there were scenes similar to these.

The British government did a certain amount to help Ireland. It provided some money to pay labourers to make roads and canals—but the men were too weak to work. Depots were set up to sell food—but the people had little money and could not afford to buy. Finally soup kitchens were established to give a bowl of thin soup and sometimes a slice of bread to all who came. It was not enough, but Charles Trevelyan, who was in charge of helping the famine victims, would do no more. He would not buy more food in England and Wales to feed the Irish because he feared that the extra demand would raise food prices in the rest of the United Kingdom, which he thought would be a 'crying injustice'. He even refused to forbid exports of grain from Ireland. As a result, throughout the famine, grain which the peasants had grown and sold to pay their rent was being shipped by corn merchants to English markets where the price was higher.

The famine had important consequences. In 1845 the population of Ireland had been about 8½ million. Perhaps as many as a million died of starvation, and about 1½ million went overseas to look for a living. Many went to England and Scotland, where they settled in towns to work in the factories, or else joined gangs of navvies who were building railways. Others went to America, where there are now more people of Irish descent than there are in Ireland itself. Many of those who emigrated had bitter memories of their sufferings, and put the blame for them on the British government and the English landlords who owned most of Ireland. This bitterness still persists.

9 A Country on the Move

Transport in 1815

By the early nineteenth century Britain had a good network of roads and canals. There were thousands of kilometres of roads. Most of the important routes were turnpikes, which were looked after by committees known as turnpike trusts. These committees, set up by Act of Parliament, were supposed to keep the roads in good repair and were allowed in return to set up gates where all road users had to pay a toll. Some turnpike trusts were able to make and maintain good smooth roads. Others found the money from tolls was not enough to keep the surface in proper repair. Travellers found that sometimes they could bowl along in fine style, but sometimes they were slowed down by ruts and pot-holes.

The roads carried a good deal of traffic. Teams of six horses hauled wagons loaded with as much as 2½ tonnes of goods, while passengers were whisked along in well-sprung coaches at an average speed of 15 kilometres an hour. Road travel was not cheap. Passengers with seats on the roof of the coach paid just over a penny a kilometre. Inside passengers paid double. The roads were dotted with inns where horses were changed, meals were served and beds provided for the weary travellers. Road transport was big business. In 1836 it was reckoned that there were about 3,000 coaches, and that 30,000 people depended on the traffic for their living.

In addition to the roads, there were 6,500 kilometres of canals and navigable rivers. One horse could pull a canal barge loaded with up to 40 tonnes of coal, manure, building materials, iron ore, china clay or other such bulky materials, at a steady 3 kilometres an hour. Many factories were built on the banks of canals and had their own private wharfs where raw materials were unloaded from the barges, and finished goods were loaded to be shipped off to their customers. Without improved roads and canals industry could not have developed as it did. But many people felt it would grow even faster if there was some means of transport to move both goods and people long distances cheaply and quickly. Railways proved to be the answer to this problem.

Early railways

Railways had been used for many years in and around coal-pits, particularly in Northumberland and Durham. In most cases, horses were used to pull the trucks along the track, but in some cases the wagons were attached to a cable which was wound in by a stationary steam-engine. Some engineers had tried to mount steam-engines on wheels, but they were so heavy that the track broke and buckled under them.

By 1820, things were different. The newest engines were much lighter and more powerful. George Stephenson, a Northumberland colliery engineer, built several 'locomotive engines' which could travel along an iron railway pulling loaded coal-trucks at up to 15 kilometres an hour. Stephenson was well known in the north-east of England, and when local mine-owners decided to make a railway to link Stockton and Darlington in County Durham, they called on him to engineer the line. The railway opened in 1825. Some trains were pulled by horses, but others were powered by steam. Their first engine, *Locomotion*, could reach 26

Toll-gates were unpopular. When tolls were increased in South Wales in 1842 gangs of men, some disguised as women, pulled the gates down. (These were the Rebecca riots)

k.p.h., but worked best at less than half that speed. As time passed, more engines and fewer horses were used and the amount of traffic increased steadily. In particular, the directors were surprised by the large number of passengers who used the new service. All this meant that the railway made large profits, which encouraged businessmen to build lines in other places.

The Manchester–Liverpool railway

The most important new railway was the Manchester to Liverpool. Once again the line was engineered by George Stephenson. Work began on the 48-kilometre route in 1826. The line was a difficult one. It crossed Chat Moss, a peat bog 6 kilometres wide, and went through Olive Mount, a great mass of hard rock. Stephenson laid a mat of heather and branches

covered with gravel over Chat Moss, and found that it easily supported the weight of a train. At Olive Mount he dug out a huge cutting, 3 kilometres long. In places it was 25 metres deep. Works like this were very expensive, and by the time it was opened in 1830, the Manchester to Liverpool railway had cost about £800,000. It was the first railway to be designed for steam traffic, and a year before it was opened, a contest was held at Rainhill to decide what kind of locomotive should be used on the line. There were four entries, and the competition was won by Stephenson's *Rocket*, which pulled a load of 13 tonnes at an average speed of 23 k.p.h. and reached a top speed of 47 k.p.h. On 15 September 1830 the railway was officially opened. It was a great day, ruined by a fatal accident. William Huskisson, the well-known MP, stepped into the path of the *Rocket* which knocked him down and crushed his leg.

He was rushed off to a nearby house by George Stephenson, driving one of his other engines, the *Northumbrian*, but he died the same night. In spite of this unfortunate beginning, the new railway prospered and the shareholders made a lot of money.

The London to Birmingham and the Great Western

The success of the Manchester to Liverpool railway led businessmen and engineers to plan other, much longer lines. For instance, George Stephenson and his son, Robert, engineered a line between London and Birmingham, a distance of 181 kilometres. This railway, which was begun in 1833 and finished in 1838, was by far the longest in Britain at the time. The total cost of the line amounted to £4½ million—nearly double the estimates made before the work was started. There were several tunnels on the route. The longest, Kilsby tunnel, was more than 2 kilometres long and cost £300,000. Meanwhile the Stephensons' great rival, Isambard Kingdom Brunel, had been working on the London to Bristol line, the Great Western Railway, which was completed in 1841 at a cost of £6½ million. The work was held up for a long time while Box tunnel, near Bath, was completed. This was 3 kilometres long, and was made by two gangs working from

Brunel was one of the most brilliant engineers of the nineteenth century. He designed railways, ships and bridges

opposite ends. When they met in the middle Brunel was so pleased that he gave his ring to the foreman of one of the gangs.

Building a railway

Making a railway was a complicated business. First, the route had to be surveyed and Parliament had to pass an Act giving permission for the line to be made. Then a company was set up to raise the necessary money. Once this had been done, the land for the line was purchased and contracters were appointed to make the line. Next gangs of labourers, known as navvies, moved in to level the line with embankments, cuttings and tunnels. Only then could the rails be laid, the stations built and the trains begin to run.

There were many snags to be overcome. Some landowners refused to allow the surveyors onto their property. In Leicestershire Lord Harborough drove them off by sending gangs of stable boys and gamekeepers armed with sticks, stones and guns to guard all the entrances to his estate. In the early days many MPs opposed railways and voted against them. Some pointed out that railways would ruin the trade of coach owners, inn-keepers and all who depended on road and canal traffic for a living. Some maintained that steam-trains would frighten cattle, ruin crops and stop game birds breeding. Others said that railway travellers would become 'heartily sick, what with foul air, smoke and sulphur'. A few argued that the human body would be unable to stand the strain of travelling at more than 40 k.p.h., so that if a train went really fast, all the passengers would die. A group of clergymen in Hampshire even petitioned against a railway because they thought country people would stay away from church to watch the trains go by.

Even when Parliament had approved the line, there was still likely to be trouble. Those who owned land along the route often charged the railway companies huge sums for the land needed to make the line. Some insisted on the line being hidden in a tunnel or a cutting, while a few demanded a private station. Once work had begun, there were always difficulties. At

Box tunnel two steam-pumps had to be set up to keep the workings dry. The navvies drilling the tunnel used a tonne of gunpowder and a tonne of candles a week, while 30 million bricks were used to line it. All these supplies had to be bought and delivered to the site, and a huge gang of navvies had to be housed and paid.

The navvies were strong and tough and worked very hard, digging, shovelling and blasting. Their work was dangerous. When making cuttings they were liable to be buried by falls of earth. In tunnelling some were drowned when underground streams suddenly broke through into the workings, while many were injured by flying stones as they blasted their way through hard rock. They were well paid—between fifteen shillings and a pound a week. They lived in turf and timber huts close to the line, and when they had a day off, they swaggered down to the nearest town or village to spend their earnings on drink. Sometimes they fought among themselves. Often they killed all the rabbits, pheasants and other game anywhere near their camps. All the people in the neighbourhood breathed a sigh of relief when the line was finished and the navvies moved on.

Many contractors found that railway-building was much more difficult than they had expected and went bankrupt. A few made huge fortunes. One of the most famous, Samuel Peto, employed 14,000 navvies, became an MP and was knighted.

The railway mania

The early railways made good profits. This led many people to believe that if they put their money into a railway they were certain to make a fortune. For a time, the whole country seemed to go 'railway mad', and whenever a company asked for money to build a new line, people rushed forward to invest. Most railway companies were honest, and hundreds of kilometres of line were laid, but there were some swindlers who saw a way to make easy money. They would propose a new railway line and advertise shares for sale in the papers. More often than not they received thousands of pounds, which

they kept. But the railway was never built. In October 1845 the price of railway shares began to fall, and those who had paid high prices for them lost huge sums of money. Yet through all this excitement, railway-building continued, and by the end of 1851 all the most important towns in Britain were linked by rail.

The railway system

The railway system grew up without any over-all plan. Each line was owned by a separate company. From the early days they co-operated to run long-distance trains which crossed the territories of several companies, and as time passed many of the small companies were taken over by larger and richer ones. George Hudson, a Yorkshire business-man, bought up line after line, until by 1848 he controlled about a third of the network and was known as the Railway King. He made a huge fortune, but in 1849 it was discovered that some of his deals had been illegal and he was forced to retire. Each company employed its own engineers. Different engineers had different ideas, and were free to try them out. For example, the Stephensons always designed railways with a gauge of 1.4125 metres (4 feet 8½ inches). Brunel favoured 2.1 metres (7 feet), the London to Colchester line was 1.50 metres (5 feet), while all Irish lines were 1.575 metres (5 feet 3 inches). Eventually, in 1846, Parliament ordered that all new lines were to be 1.4125 metres, but it was not until 1892 that all the old Great Western track was converted to the narrow gauge.

Passenger traffic

All railways carried passengers, who were divided into three classes. First-class passengers sat in comfort on padded seats in enclosed carriages. Second-class passengers sat crowded together on hard wooden benches in open-sided coaches. Third-class passengers had to stand in open trucks. Fortunately railway engines burned coke, so there was never much smoke, but there was plenty of steam, sparks and fumes to blow into the faces of the third-

Glasgow

EDINBURGH

Newcastle

Carlisle Durham Stockton

York

Preston
Liverpool Manchester

Chester Derby

Birmingham Rugby

LONDON

Bristol Dover

Southampton

Brighton

0 50 km

N

class passengers. Many trains only had first- and second-class coaches. On the Great Western, only night trains had any accommodation for third-class passengers, who had to stand all the way on a slow train open to the wind and weather. All this changed in 1844, when Parliament passed an Act ordering railways to run at least one train every day to carry third-class passengers in covered coaches with seats. These 'parliamentary' trains had to stop at every station and average at least 20 k.p.h. The third-class fare was not to be more than a penny a mile.

Effects of railways

Railways made it quicker and cheaper to transport both goods and passengers. In 1851 a writer pointed out that a London businessman could catch a train at Euston at 5 p.m., travel smoothly to Manchester for his supper, spend the next day choosing and buying bales of cloth in some cotton spinner's warehouse, travel back to London for his evening meal and be certain that the goods he had chosen would be delivered to his office next morning. Countrymen, too, benefited. One Northamptonshire farmer used to visit Smithfield market in London every week. Before the railway opened the round trip took three and a half days and cost three pounds four shillings in coach fares alone. By rail the journey took three hours each way and the first-class return fare was less than two pounds. What was more, the farmer knew that any produce he sent to London by rail would still be fresh and fit for sale when it arrived.

Railways also made it easier for people to travel to and from their work. Businessmen began to move out of industrial towns and set up house in the country, close to a railway station. At weekends and holiday time, on the other hand, town workers used the railways to go out and enjoy the seaside and the countryside. Before the railways, travel had been too expensive for most working people, but now they were able to save a little money and go on rail excursions to holiday centres like Brighton and Blackpool, which grew and prospered as a result. But for some people the railways meant ruin. Once a line had opened, coach services had to close down, and so did many of the old coaching-inns. Canal proprietors did better. As a rule they were able to compete with the railways by cutting their prices, and remained in business well into the twentieth century.

Railways also altered the landscape. On the outskirts of towns new station buildings were erected which were often very large and imposing, while in the countryside many valleys were dominated by huge bridges which carried the tracks across them. Until the coming of the railways most people had seen nothing larger or faster than a horse and cart. The sight of a steam-engine hauling a train of coaches at more than 40 k.p.h. across such a bridge must have made them feel that a new age had dawned.

The post and telegraph

Postal services benefited greatly from the growth of the railway system. Up to 1840, post was carried on horseback or by coach. The cost of sending a letter depended on the number of sheets of paper and the distance it had to travel. It cost one shilling and four pence to send one sheet from London to Edinburgh. Two sheets cost two shillings and eight pence, and so on. An envelope counted as an extra sheet. The postage fee was paid on delivery. This system was cumbersome and expensive to operate. Many letters were carried to their destinations and then destroyed undelivered because the person to whom they were addressed refused to pay. Rowland Hill, a civil servant, suggested that all letters should be charged the same amount, no matter how far they were carried.

The impressive facade of the London terminus of the South-Eastern Railway

An engine pulling passenger coaches crosses a viaduct on the Sheffield to Manchester Railway

The postage fee was to be paid by the sender, by means of a small stamp which he would buy at a post office and stick on the letter. In 1840 Hill's idea was introduced. All letters were charged a penny. The result of the penny post was a huge increase in the number of letters, and the railways were used to carry them.

Railways also helped in the development of the telegraph. In 1837 scientists had developed a method of sending messages along wires using electric current from a battery. In 1838 the system was tried out along a short stretch of the Great Western Railway so that one station master could tell the next that a train was on its way. The system became famous in 1845 when it helped to catch a murderer, John Tawell, who had poisoned his mistress. Her screams alarmed the neighbours, who at once informed the police. Tawell gave them the slip, but was seen boarding a London train at Slough station. His description was at once telegraphed to Paddington, and when he arrived there, he found the police waiting for him. In 1844 Parliament ordered all railways to install the system and in 1851 a telegraph cable was laid across the Channel. The process continued. In 1866 Europe and America were linked by cable and by 1872 telegraphic messages could be sent to Australia.

Developments in shipping

At the beginning of the nineteenth century all long sea voyages had to be made in wooden sailing-ships. A few steamships had been built, but they were used only on canal and river trips. Gradually steamships improved. In 1816 the first steam Channel-crossing was made. In 1819 the *Rob Roy* was launched at Dunbarton. She was 24 metres long and was reliable enough to be used on a regular passenger service from Dover to Calais. In the same year the *Savannah*, an American sailing-ship fitted with a steam-engine, sailed across the Atlantic, but for most of the voyage she relied on her sails. The steam-engine was only started when the wind dropped.

All early steamships were paddle-steamers with wooden hulls. Their range was limited because the engines used so much fuel that on a long voyage all the cargo space would be taken up with coal for the engines. Brunel was the first person to see a way round this problem. He realised that a very large ship would be much more economical than a small one.* He there-

* In mathematical terms, the power needed to drive a ship increases as the square of its dimensions, while its carrying capacity increases as their cube.

fore set to work to build the biggest ship in the world. The result was the *Great Western*, a wooden paddle-steamer, 71.6 metres long, powered by two Maudslay steam-engines producing 750 horse power. The ship was designed to carry passengers across the Atlantic, and had comfortable cabins and a splendid saloon. It went into service in 1838 and made nearly seventy Atlantic crossings, taking about two weeks for each voyage.

The *Great Western* was a success, and Brunel decided to build another, even larger ship. This was the *Great Britain*, 87.5 metres long, which went into service in 1845. It was a much more advanced ship that the *Great Western*. It had an iron hull. Small iron-built ships had been used for river traffic since 1822, but Brunel was the first person to make a huge ocean-going vessel out of iron. The *Great Britain* was driven, not by paddles, but by a screw propellor. The first propellor-driven ship had been launched in 1838 and performed so well that Brunel at once decided to use the new system in his great ship. The Admiralty was not so sure. But when a screw-driven sloop, the *Rattler*, beat a paddle-driven boat of the same size and power in a

tug-of-war, the navy decided to build screw steamers. Meanwhile, passengers crossing the Atlantic were quite used to travelling in a screw-driven, iron steamship. It was a great improvement on the earlier sailing-ships.

The Great Exhibition

At the beginning of 1851 Britons were in a mood to celebrate. The *Spectator* magazine looked back over the years since 1800 and declared:

> We have gained freedom. Food, clothes and lodging are cheaper. The factory system dresses the women of the working class like the ladies of the last century.

During the same period 'railways, steamships, electric telegraphs, photography and chloroform' had all been introduced. It was clear that on the whole life was much better in 1850 than it had been fifty years before. To celebrate the progress which had been made, it was decided to hold a great international exhibition in Hyde Park in London.

The organisers had two aims. They wanted

The **Great Britain** *was launched at Bristol in 1843. In 1970 her hull was brought back to Bristol, where she is being refitted*

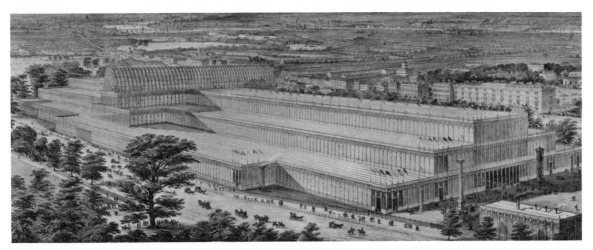

This 'aeronautic' view of the Crystal Palace gives a good idea of the great size of the building

people to see all the marvels that had been produced by the hard work and careful thought of engineers and artists all over the world, and in addition, they hoped that the exhibition might persuade the nations of the world that instead of going to war they should compete peacefully to produce better goods. Some people thought the whole thing would be a waste of time and money but the idea was supported by Prince Albert, Queen Victoria's husband, and by many British manufacturers, who were certain that their products would be much better than those from other countries.

The Crystal Palace

There were many problems to be overcome before the exhibition could be mounted. The most difficult was to design a suitable building. It had to be big enough to house all the exhibits and yet be quick and easy to put up. In the end the winning design was sent in by Joseph Paxton, the Duke of Devonshire's head gardener. He suggested a building like a huge greenhouse, with a cast-iron framework. The work went on through the winter and spring of 1851 and by the end of April the 'Crystal Palace' was complete. It was vast. It was 578 metres long, and 34 metres high at the highest point. It contained nearly 90,000 square metres of glass and covered more than 7 hectares. By 1 May 1851 the 13,000 exhibitors—half of whom came

from Britain and the Empire—had moved in and arranged their exhibits, and all was ready for the official opening.

The exhibition was opened by Queen Victoria accompanied by Prince Albert. Half a million people crammed into Hyde Park to see the fun while the Crystal Palace itself was crowded with invited ticket holders. Albert made a speech. The queen replied. The Archbishop of Canterbury said a prayer. A huge choir, accompanied by five organs, sang Handel's 'Hallelujah Chorus' and the queen, seated on a crimson throne, declared the exhibition open. Attendants removed the boundary ropes, and the ticket holders pushed and jostled in their haste to see round the huge pavilion.

The exhibits

The visitors were very impressed. The Crystal Palace itself was a marvel. It was so large and lofty that some huge elm trees growing in the park were enclosed in it like greenhouse plants. Yet it was light, sparkling and airy. There was no building like it anywhere else in the world. Then there were the exhibits. In the centre stood the crystal fountain, a mass of crystal glass standing more than 8 metres high, and weighing 4 tonnes. The other exhibits were divided into four classes: raw materials, machinery, manufactured goods and fine arts. Among the raw materials were huge blocks of

The latest cotton-spinning machines were on view at the Great Exhibition

copper ore from the United States, and heaps of timber from Canada, but these did not seem anything like so impressive as the machinery exhibits.

There was no doubt that the machinery from Britain compared very well with that from any other country. The crowds could admire Daniel Gooch's express locomotive , *Lord of the Isles*, built for the broad-gauge Great Western Railway. Its driving wheels were 2½ metres in diameter, and with its green paint and polished metal-work, it towered over all the other engines on display. Nearby stood James Nasmyth's huge steam-hammer, originally designed to forge the drive shaft of Brunel's ship, the *Great Britain*. Nasmyth claimed that his hammer was so easily controlled that it could deliver a blow of 500 tonnes, or, if required, lightly crack an eggshell. Further on was

Applegarth's vertical printing-press, capable of turning out 10,000 sheets of the *Illustrated London News* every hour. All these were British products, but many landowners were interested in an American exhibit, McCormick's mechanical reaper, which could, it was said, cut an acre (just under half a hectare) of grain an hour.

The greatest variety of exhibits was to be seen among the manufactured goods, which ranged from sideboards and pianos to watches and rubber boats. There was a watch the size of a pea, and a copper bath complete with a shower and a stove to heat the water. Few exhibits were plain or simple in design. Most of them were smothered in carvings and decoration. In years gone by craftsmen had laboured for hours to carve out the decoration on pieces of furniture. Now it was done in minutes by a machine. Most Victorians admired this elaborate machine-made decoration. Only a few disagreed. One critic wrote of 'the prodigious ugliness' of much of the exhibition, while William Morris, a seventeen-year-old, later to become famous as a designer, was 'aghast' at the 'heaviness' and 'tastelessness' of the objects on display.

In the fine arts section, there were many statues, dominated by a zinc figure of Queen Victoria nearly 7 metres high. The best-liked statue was the 'Greek Slave' by Hiram Powers, an American sculptor. This depicted 'a young and beautiful Greek girl, deprived of her clothes and exposed for sale to some wealthy Eastern barbarian'. A female figure on horseback fighting off a ferocious tiger was also very popular, while many visitors liked a pathetic figure of a small boy weeping over his broken drum. Most of the statues tried to copy the style of classical Greek and Roman figures and were quite unoriginal. By the time a visitor had looked at every one of the 16 kilometres of displays he would be ready to visit the refreshment rooms, where he could buy bread, cakes, pickles, ham, coffee and mineral water. Toilets were also provided, and by the time the exhibition closed more than 800,000 people had paid to use them.

Summing up

The exhibition was a great success. 'I never remember,' wrote Queen Victoria, 'anything before that everyone was so pleased with, as is the case with this exhibition.' At first the admission fee was £1. Later it was reduced to five shillings and, on some days, to one shilling. On the 'shilling days' the exhibition was packed with crowds of working people, many of whom had come to London from the country on special excursion trains. Some Londoners had feared disorder and drunkeness on such occasions, but the crowds behaved just as well as on other days. On 15 October 1851, the exhibition was closed. Six million visitors had paid to see it, and it made a profit of £186,000. Most of this was used to buy land at South Kensington on which a number of museums and colleges now

The 'Greek Slave'—the most popular statue in the exhibition

stand. Joseph Paxton, the designer of the Crystal Palace, received £5,000 and a knighthood. With the exhibition such a success, Britain seemed satisfied and at peace as 1851 ended. 'We have,' said the *Manchester Guardian* in December, 'as much, if not more reason for contentment and thankfulness,' as 'at the close of any past year in our history.' Most of the newspaper's middle-class readers would have agreed. But workers living in cramped houses in stinking industrial towns were neither contented nor thankful. Indeed, many of them felt that they had no future in Britain and went to start a new life in the United States and Canada.

Index